Common
Occupational
Readiness
Essentials

CERTIFICATION PREP

Adobe
Illustrator
Creative Cloud

by

D. Michael Ploor, MBA
National Board Certified Teacher
STEM Curriculum Integration Specialist
School District of Hillsborough County
Tampa, Florida

Publisher
The Goodheart-Willcox Company, Inc.
Tinley Park, Illinois
www.g-w.com

Copyright © 2018
by
The Goodheart-Willcox Company, Inc.

Previous edition copyright 2017.

All rights reserved. No part of this work may be reproduced, stored, or transmitted
in any form or by any electronic or mechanical means, including information storage
and retrieval systems, without the prior written permission of
The Goodheart-Willcox Company, Inc.

Manufactured in the United States of America.

ISBN: 978-1-63126-855-7

5 6 7 8 9 – 18 – 21

The Goodheart-Willcox Company, Inc., Brand Disclaimer: Brand names, company names, and
illustrations for products and services included in this text are provided for educational purposes only
and do not represent or imply endorsement or recommendation by the author or the publisher.

The Goodheart-Willcox Company, Inc., Safety Notice: The reader is expressly advised to carefully read,
understand, and apply all safety precautions and warnings described in this book or that might also be
indicated in undertaking the activities and exercises described herein to minimize risk of personal injury
or injury to others. Common sense and good judgment should also be exercised and applied to help
avoid all potential hazards. The reader should always refer to the appropriate manufacturer's technical
information, directions, and recommendations; then proceed with care to follow specific equipment
operating instructions. The reader should understand these notices and cautions are not exhaustive.

The publisher makes no warranty or representation whatsoever, either expressed or implied, including
but not limited to equipment, procedures, and applications described or referred to herein, their quality,
performance, merchantability, or fitness for a particular purpose. The publisher assumes no responsibility
for any changes, errors, or omissions in this book. The publisher specifically disclaims any liability
whatsoever, including any direct, indirect, incidental, consequential, special, or exemplary damages
resulting, in whole or in part, from the reader's use or reliance upon the information, instructions,
procedures, warnings, cautions, applications or other matter contained in this book. The publisher
assumes no responsibility for the activities of the reader.

Cover image: photolinc/Shutterstock.com

Table of Contents

Lesson 1   *Elements of Art and Principles of Design* 5

Lesson 2   *Color Models, Images, and Fonts* 18

Lesson 3   *Digital-Project Management* . . . 27

Lesson 4   *Illustrator Interface* 34

Lesson 5   *Vector Images* 61

Lesson 6   *Gradients* 80

Lesson 7   *Vector Image Conversion* 101

Lesson 8   *Text and Templates* 119

Copyright Goodheart-Willcox Co., Inc.   For individual use only—reproduction or duplication of this copyrighted material is prohibited.

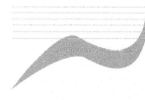

Introduction

The Common Occupational Readiness Essentials (CORE) series of certification preparation guides focuses on mastering the essential basic skills needed as a workplace-ready user of the software. The goal of each CORE certification preparation guide is to provide practice in each essential basic skill required by employers who use the software. To prove workplace readiness, you will also be prepared to take the official certification exam for the software.

CORE Adobe Illustrator Creative Cloud will help prepare you to take the Adobe Certified Associate (ACA) Adobe Illustrator Creative Cloud certification exam. It provides step-by-step instruction for the features and commands covered on the certification exam. The focus of the lessons is to practice *using* the actual commands and features instead of creating a complete end product. Most lesson content is created using the software, and minimal downloading of files is required. Furthermore, each certification preparation guide is broken down into small learning units to enable better comprehension and application of the software. Where required, answers are provided at the back of the certification preparation guide.

Certification as an Adobe Certified Associate demonstrates an aptitude with Adobe software. ACA certification is offered for Adobe Dreamweaver, Adobe Flash, Adobe Photoshop, Adobe Premier, Adobe Illustrator, and Adobe InDesign. Certification exams are provided by Certiport, Inc., through various testing facilities. Visit www.certiport.com for more information on registering for certification exams.

About the Author

D. Michael Ploor is the author of the CORE series of certification preparation guides. Mr. Ploor's students have achieved exceptional results with the CORE certification preparation guides. His students collectively pass more than 500 industry certification exams each year without the need for other preparation materials. Mr. Ploor has demonstrated the strength of integrating the CORE guides in a diverse mix of courses.

Mr. Ploor is also the author of three textbooks on the subject of video game design: *Introduction to Video Game Design, Video Game Design Foundations,* and *Video Game Design Composition.* He is a National Board Certified Teacher in Career and Technical Education and holds an MBA degree from the University of South Florida. He maintains professional teaching credentials in Business Education and Education Media Specialist.

Mr. Ploor is at the forefront of innovative teaching and curriculum. He developed STEM curriculum while serving as the lead teacher in the Career Academy of Computer Game Design at Middleton Magnet STEM High School. Mr. Ploor has applied his skills as a STEM Curriculum Integration Specialist in designing innovative curriculum and by collaborating to construct the state standards for video game design in several states. He has also been instrumental in authoring competitive events for Career and Technical Student Organizations such as the Future Business Leaders of America (FBLA) and Phi Beta Lambda (PBL).

In addition to publishing textbooks and lessons, Mr. Ploor provides professional development as a frequent presenter at regional and national conferences to promote CTE education and video game design curriculum.

For individual use only—reproduction or duplication of this copyrighted material is prohibited.   Copyright Goodheart-Willcox Co., Inc.

Lesson 1
Elements of Art and Principles of Design

Objectives

Students will compare and contrast traditional artwork and digital artwork. Students will describe the seven elements of art. Students will apply the principles of design.

Introduction to Traditional and Digital Artwork

Artwork is an artistic work developed using a combination of art elements to create a visual scene, character, volume, or image. *Traditional artwork* is created without the use of computer technology. Examples of traditional artwork include paintings, drawings, sculptures, pottery, and so on. *Digital artwork* is created using a computer. The artist inputs information into a computer program that helps create the artwork. The final artwork can be displayed in physical form or in virtual form. Digital artwork can be output in physical form such as a printed page or an object produced by molding, rapid prototyping machine, computer-guided lathe, or other computer-controlled output. Digital artwork in virtual form may be digital pictures or animations displayed on a computer screen.

Whether the artist is working with virtual media like a video game or physical media like a sculpture, the elements of art and principles of design hold true. Thousands of years of trial and error by artists have established these universal truths.

The *elements of art* deal with the individual features needed to compose artwork. Each individual feature or element is constructed and arranged to create artwork. Artwork should also be developed following the principles of design. The *principles of design* govern how to effectively combine the elements of art to compose a pleasing work of art.

Elements of Art

There are seven elements of art: shape, form, line, color, value, space, and texture. Each of these elements details an aspect of a single attribute of an object. These elements are universal and apply to both traditional and digital art. Below are brief descriptions of each element of art.

Copyright Goodheart-Willcox Co., Inc.   For individual use only—reproduction or duplication of this copyrighted material is prohibited.

Shape

The black circle shown in **Figure 1-1** is a shape defined by the edges of the black ink on the paper. Shape is a defined area in two-dimensional space. Shapes come in two different varieties: geometric and organic.

Geometric shapes are regular figures, like a square, circle, triangle, octagon, or trapezoid. Geometric shapes are also known as 2D primitives. *Primitives* are regular shapes and objects that are used to assemble more complex shapes or objects. For example, the robotic character shown in **Figure 1-1** is constructed from 2D primitives: three circles, five rectangles, and one trapezoid.

Irregular shapes are known as *organic shapes.* Organic shapes describe things like a cloud, tree, blowing steam, or even an ergonomic computer mouse. Mostly, organic shapes are used to describe things in nature. In practice, organic shapes describe natural and unnatural shapes that have curved or irregular edges.

Form

The assembly of 2D shapes to represent a third dimension is *form.* Form shows measurable dimensions of length, width, and depth for an object. A traditional sculpture has form, but a computer-modeled character also has form.

Line

If you look at the basic robot in **Figure 1-1,** each shape is defined by the boundary created by a solid black line. A line is the path between two points and is most often used as a boundary to create a shape. Lines can be straight, curved, looping, or organic and can be solid or composed of dashes or other marks.

When a line is composed of dashes or other marks, it is an implied line, as shown in **Figure 1-2.** An *implied line* is the path the viewer's eye takes to connect the two endpoints of the line when it is not continuous. Basically, the viewer's eye connects the dots with an invisible (implied) line to complete the line path.

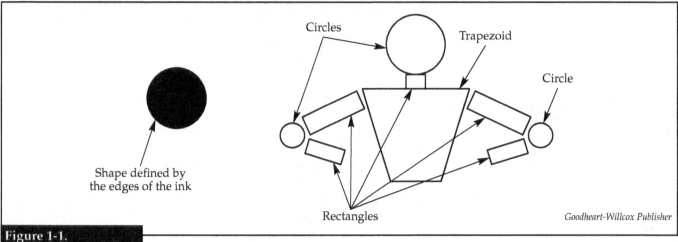

Circles   Trapezoid   Circle

Shape defined by the edges of the ink

Rectangles

Goodheart-Willcox Publisher

Figure 1-1.

Simple shapes can be used to create a basic figure.

For individual use only—reproduction or duplication of this copyrighted material is prohibited.   Copyright Goodheart-Willcox Co., Inc.

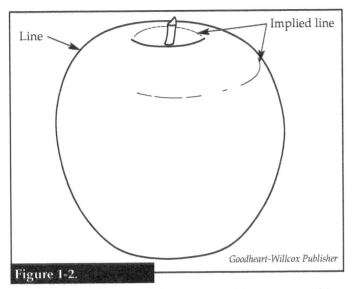

Figure 1-2.

Both lines and implied lines are used to compose this apple.

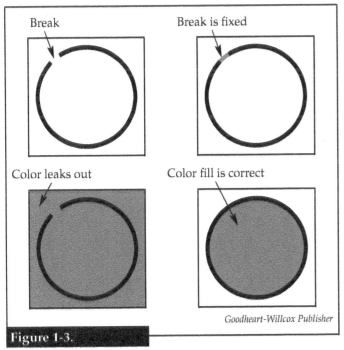

Figure 1-3.

In most imaging software, a shape must be fully enclosed by a line in order to be filled.

Color

The combination of hues applied to a line or shape is its color. *Hue* is the pure color. Hue can be tinted or shaded to add additional colors. A *tint* is a hue with white added. A *shade* is a hue with black added. Tinted colors are lighter and shaded colors are darker than the hue. A *tone* is a hue with both black and white, or gray, added.

In imaging software, the *line color* or *outline color* is applied to the border line only. The *shape color* or *shape fill* is color applied to the shape defined by the line. In most imaging software, the shape color can be applied only if the shape is completely enclosed by lines or the edges of other shapes. If there is a break in the line or the shape is not completely enclosed, the color will "leak out," as shown in **Figure 1-3.**

A color wheel illustrates the relationship of primary, secondary, and tertiary colors, as shown in **Figure 1-4.** *Primary colors* are red, yellow, and blue. All other colors are created from the three primary colors. *Secondary colors* are created by blending two primary colors. *Tertiary colors* are created by blending a primary and a secondary color or two secondary colors. *Analogous* colors appear adjacent to each other on the color wheel. Red, orange, and yellow are analogous colors, and they appear in a group on the same side of the color wheel. *Complementary* colors are opposite each other on the color wheel. Complementary colors create high contrast. Purple is a complementary color to yellow. Yellow text will be easily seen if it is placed on a purple background.

Value

Value is the use of light and dark to add highlight, shading, or shadows. If you look at a *monochromatic* image, which is an image with one hue, the entire image is created based on the principle of value. Look at the image of the apple shown in **Figure 1-5.** By using just the black hue, the image can have shape, line, and value. Value of the black hue is shades of gray. Depth is created around the stem of the apple by darkening that area. Near the top of the apple, depth is created by lightening the part of the apple that is closest to the light.

All objects shown on a computer screen are composed of pixels, or picture elements. *Pixels* are the smallest areas of illumination on an electronic display. In digital artwork, artists use pixel shading to add to the illusion of depth. *Pixel shading* is the use of lighter and darker colors, or changes in value, to create light and shadow. As objects get farther from the light source, the objects are darkened so they appear farther from the source.

Copyright Goodheart-Willcox Co., Inc.   For individual use only—reproduction or duplication of this copyrighted material is prohibited.

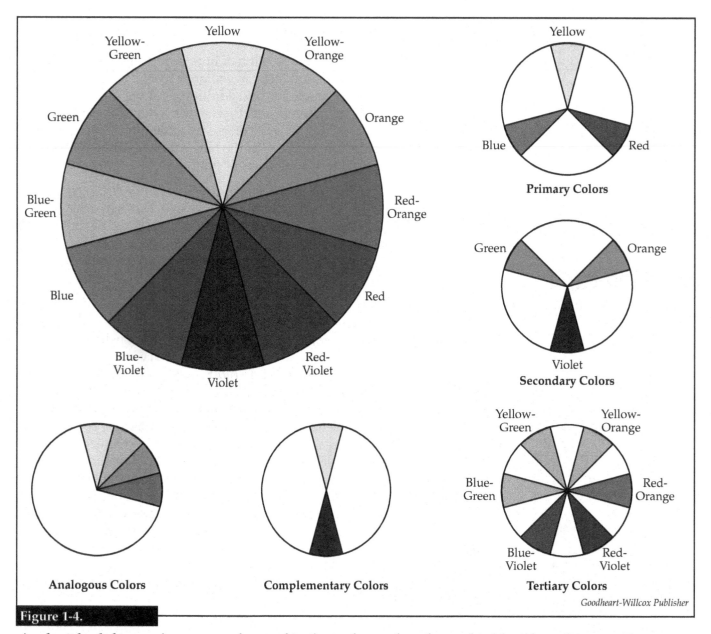

A color wheel shows primary, secondary, and tertiary colors and can be used to identify analogous and complementary colors. Refer to the color wheel image file on the student companion website.

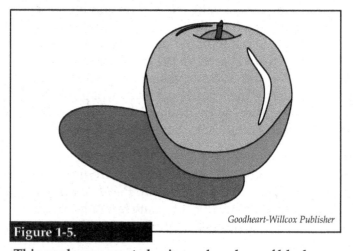

Goodheart-Willcox Publisher

Figure 1-5.

This apple was created using only values of black.

Space

The area or volume in a scene is the space. Space may be physical or virtual. A sculpture occupies physical space. An artist actually cuts into the block of marble and creates a statue with physical length, width, and depth. However, using a computer, an artist can create in virtual space. The object created in a 3D modeling program has virtual length, width, and depth. In 2D art, whether physical or virtual, space must be represented with illusion.

Positive and negative space apply emphasis to the design. *Positive space* is the area or volume occupied by the primary objects. *Negative space* is

Copyright Goodheart-Willcox Co., Inc.

the area or volume around or between the primary objects. An example of these can be found in a portrait photograph. You are the positive space. The volume between you and the background is the negative space. The amount of negative space in a design can help provide contrast and emphasis to the primary objects. Imagine the portrait is taken as a panoramic view in a stadium. While you are still a primary object, you are surrounded by hundreds of other objects. You are hard to identify as the primary object in the photograph. This is because there is little negative space to separate you from everything else. Without any negative space, your image has less emphasis than it did in the portrait of just you in front of a background. A scene can become cluttered if there is not enough negative space.

In three-dimensional space, length, width, and depth dimensions are used to create an object. When working with a 2D surface like a sheet of paper or a computer screen, the artist must trick the eye to create the illusion of 3D space. In computer rendering, artists apply both pixel shading and vertex shading to help create the illusion of 3D. *Vertex shading* is moving the points on an object to resize it such that the object appears smaller in the distance. The principle of visual perspective is applied during vertex shading.

Visual perspective is the proportional scaling of objects as they move toward a vanishing point. In **Figure 1-6,** notice how the parallel lines of the path angle inward until the lines meet in the distance. Of course, the sides of the path remain parallel. It is just the principle of visual perspective that makes the sides of the path appear to converge. Also, notice how the tree trunks appear to get thinner in the distance. Each object is scaled down as it moves toward the vanishing point. The point where receding parallel lines appear to meet is the *vanishing point.* There may be one, two, or three vanishing points, but one- and two-point perspectives are the most common. A two-point perspective is shown in the drawing in **Figure 1-6.**

Also notice in **Figure 1-6** that the trees closest to the viewer appear to be in focus, while the trees in the distance appear out of focus. This effect can be applied in artwork to help enhance the illusion of depth. By adding a blur effect to an object in the distance, the spatial relationship of near or distant objects is enhanced. The spatial relationship describes how an object appears in space in relation to the viewer.

Texture

Variations in form and color create texture, which is an uneven surface. *Tactile texture* is an irregular surface that can be physically felt, like sandpaper. When you touch it, you feel the surface is bumpy or rough. This texture is a variation in surface depth to create a coarse physical sensation. *Optical texture* is creating variation in what you see. The skin of an orange has an optical texture because the color changes around the orange. The surface of the orange is not a single solid color. Additionally, the orange has tactile texture because the surface has physical bumps that can be felt.

Principles of Design

The principles of design are the set of rules or guidelines used to create artwork. The principles of design are specific to make sure you are creating effective layouts or art. Depending on the type of design (web, game, fine art, or other), the number

Copyright Goodheart-Willcox Co., Inc.   For individual use only—reproduction or duplication of this copyrighted material is prohibited.

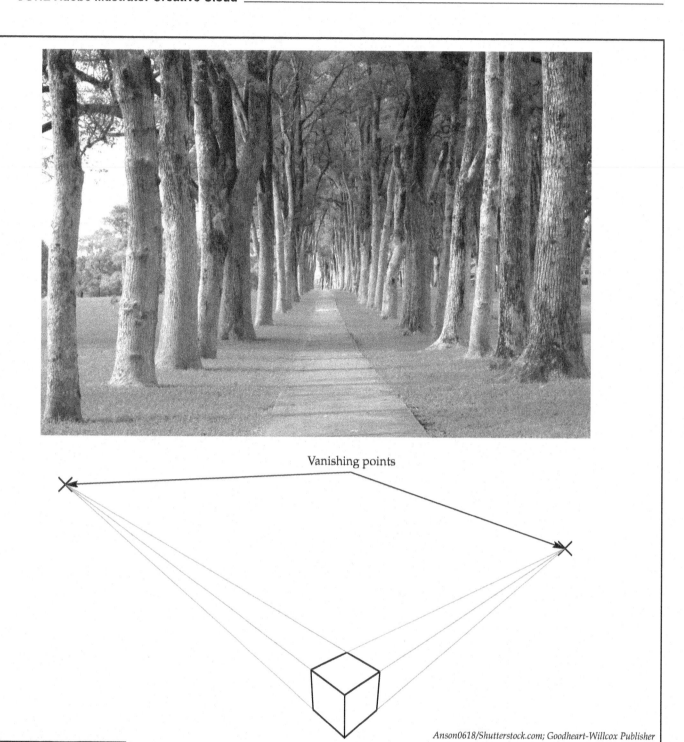

Vanishing points

Anson0618/Shutterstock.com; Goodheart-Willcox Publisher

Figure 1-6.

The edges of the path and the rows of trees appear to converge at a single vanishing point.

of principles will change. For most digital design projects, the principles of design are movement, emphasis, harmony, variety, balance, contrast, proportion, pattern, and unity.

Movement

Applied action is *movement.* In traditional art forms, a static picture must convey movement. Often in digital art, movement is done through animation. However, an

For individual use only—reproduction or duplication of this copyrighted material is prohibited.

Copyright Goodheart-Willcox Co., Inc.

Figure 1-7.

Communicate movement

Clipart.com

Even though this image is not moving, movement is communicated.

artist must understand and apply the movement principle even if the object is going to be animated.

Look at **Figure 1-7** and see how movement is represented in the illustration. The tassels on the jacket are drawn to the right instead of straight down. This implies the snowboarder is moving to the left. Additionally, bits of snow are drawn to the right of the snowboarder, which also imply movement to the left. Lines are added to imply movement. Straight lines imply the leftward movement, while curved lines imply the legs and outstretched arm are moving. Finally, the position of the snowboarder implies movement. For the snowboarder to be in that pose, it is logical to interpret movement, and the fact that the character is looking to the left implies leftward movement.

Emphasis

When a designer draws attention to an object, the object is given *emphasis.* Emphasis can be achieved by making an object larger, brighter, repeated, or moving. The idea behind adding emphasis is that the viewer will understand the object is special in some way in relation to other objects in the scene.

Harmony

Using similar elements is the principle of *harmony.* Harmony helps hold the image or scene together. Imagine a dirty character dressed in old raggedy clothes, but wearing a gold crown. The gold crown just does not fit with the way the character is dressed. The design of this character is not demonstrating harmony. Likewise, the elements of a scene need to have harmony. Objects that are out of place, such as a cell phone in a scene of an 18th century café, detract from the experience of the viewer.

Variety

The purposeful absence of harmony to create visual or contextual interest is the principle of *variety* (also known as alternation). This differs from emphasis in that the design is less obvious. It takes keen observations or thinking by the viewer to discover the cue. Without variety, artwork may be boring and lacking visual interest.

Balance

Objects arranged such that no one section overpowers any other part is called *balance.* When constructing a work of art, the artist needs to divide the canvas into equal parts to measure balance. Balance can be established as either symmetrical or asymmetrical, as shown in **Figure 1-8.**

Copyright Goodheart-Willcox Co., Inc.　　　　　For individual use only—reproduction or duplication of this copyrighted material is prohibited.

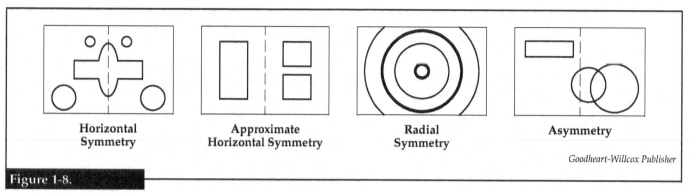

Horizontal Symmetry   Approximate Horizontal Symmetry   Radial Symmetry   Asymmetry

Goodheart-Willcox Publisher

Figure 1-8.

Symmetry and asymmetry can be used in graphic design.

Symmetrical Balance

When the right and left sides, top and bottom, or all sides are equal, *symmetrical balance,* or formal balance, is created. If the image is split down the middle, both halves contain the same number and size of objects. An example of symmetrical balance is your eyes on your face. Your nose is in the center, and one eye on each side of your nose provides symmetrical balance. Since the right side of your face is a mirror image of the left side, this is called *horizontal symmetry.* Symmetry can also be established from a center point and radiate equally from that center. *Radial symmetry* is equal in length from a center point. An example of radial symmetry is the rings created by dropping a pebble into a puddle.

Asymmetrical Balance

Asymmetrical balance, or informal balance, is the use of similar objects to create balance, or the use of color and light balance instead of object balance. Unlike symmetrical balance in which the right and left sides may be mirror images, asymmetrical balance can be seen in something like a bookshelf. The shelves balance the amount of space taken up by the books, but the size, shape, color, and arrangement of the books differs on each shelf. The concept is that a lot of something small can balance a little of something big. A swarm of small bees provides asymmetrical balance to a single large beehive. This can work with color as well, where a small area of a vibrant color provides asymmetrical balance to a large area of a neutral color.

Asymmetrical balance is often confused with asymmetry. *Asymmetry* means that the work is not at all balanced. Placing objects off-center or heavy to one side of a work can draw the viewer to an area of attention, as shown in **Figure 1-8.**

Proximity

The final element of balance is proximity. *Proximity* is how closely objects are arranged. In a social setting, placing characters close to each other conveys a meaning such as friendship or family. Conversely, placing characters far apart conveys a meaning such as enemy, stranger, or rival. Proximity can help create tension. Placing an object such as a stick of dynamite near an open fire creates tension as these two elements will cause an explosion if combined. Proximity can also help show scale or relative size. Placing a character next to a doorway provides scale to the height of the character.

For individual use only—reproduction or duplication of this copyrighted material is prohibited.   Copyright Goodheart-Willcox Co., Inc.

Rule of Thirds

The rule of thirds can be used to help achieve balance. The *rule of thirds* is a guideline that states an image should be divided into three sections horizontally and three sections vertically to create nine areas. This is like putting a tic-tac-toe board on top of the image. Where the lines cross are the focal points for a scene. Placing the objects you want the viewer to focus on at these points will draw the viewer's eye to those objects.

Contrast

The variation of color and brightness to make objects stand out from each other is *contrast*. Imagine placing blue text on a blue background. The viewer would not be able to read the letters. The designer needs to select a color, such as yellow or orange, that contrasts with the blue background. Alternately, the brightness of the blue used for either the text or background can be varied to provide contrast. Light blue text on a dark blue background may provide enough contrast for the viewer to read the words. This same principle applies to objects. Imagine using a red ball on a red background. The ball needs to contrast with the background to be seen easily.

Paolo Gianti/Shutterstock.com

Figure 1-9.

The dome in this photograph does not exist. It is a painting created to fool the viewer's eye.

Proportion

Proportion is the size of an object in relation to the other objects around it. Proportion may be exaggerated to make something more noticeable or prominent or reduced to make it more subtle. To create a realistic scene, the designer will try to show objects in proper proportion to the other objects in the scene as much as possible.

Proportion is also used to give the illusion of depth, or a third dimension. The concept of visual perspective states that an object looks smaller in the distance and gets larger as it approaches the viewer. In the Renaissance period of art, the concept of trompe l'oeil was applied to art. *Trompe l'oeil* translates to "fool the eye." Art of this type uses perspective, depth, and shadow to create ultrarealistic scenes. **Figure 1-9** shows the ceiling of the Jesuitenkirche (Jesuit church) in Vienna, Austria. The artist has made it appear as if there is a dome, but the dome does not exist. A painting of the trompe l'oeil type appears to the viewer as if looking out of a window at a real landscape or object.

Pattern

When an element is repeated, a *pattern* is created. Patterns occur in both visual layout and in motion. Visually, pattern is applied in one of three ways: regular, flowing, and progressive.

Copyright Goodheart-Willcox Co., Inc.   For individual use only—reproduction or duplication of this copyrighted material is prohibited.

Pixel Europe/Shutterstock.com

Figure 1-10.

This static two-dimensional image communicates not only movement, but depth.

A regular pattern has repeating objects of similar size and spacing, such as seen on a checkerboard. Flowing patterns have more organic shapes than regular patterns and mimic movement, as shown in **Figure 1-10.** A simple example of flowing pattern is an arrow or curve that leads to a point. The eye follows the curve from the thickest end to the point, which provides a feeling of movement or motion. Progressive patterns display a sequence or series of steps. This is a visual pattern used in animations. In static (not animated) art, a progressive pattern can simulate continuing motion or progression within a single frame, such as the image shown in **Figure 1-10.**

In animations, such as on websites, objects move in patterns. For example, if the animation is of a character running across the top of a web page as a background image scrolls, the artist must balance the pace of the animation with the movement of the background. If these are not synchronized, the animation will appear odd to the viewer.

Unity

All of the elements and principles of art work together to create unity. When something has *unity*, it appears as a single piece and not an assembly of different parts. The easiest way to explain this is to look at a character, such as Indiana Jones. The Indy character has a hat, whip, leather jacket, over-the-shoulder bag, fedora, dungarees, and boots. Each of these pieces is one part of the whole. When these pieces come together, a single character is created that has a sense of unity.

Unity also applies to the layout of a scene. Each component of the scene should look like it fits with the others. Many times, the unity of the entire project is overlooked. For example, on a multipage website the designer should strive for *site-wide consistency.* The color, layout, and location of buttons should be the same on each page. Imagine how frustrating it would be if the Home button were in a different place on each page of the website. Also, colors should be maintained to increase consistency. By adding unity elements to each page, the site feels like a single document. Without unity, the user may feel like he or she is jumping from one website to another.

Maintaining unity in the graphic design of a game, website, or user interface has the benefits of shorter development time, easier maintenance, and improved usability. Using the same items such as navigation buttons will shorten development time by not having to design new buttons for every page or level. Using copy and paste to add the same button to a different page is much faster than creating a new button. This also ensures the button is exactly the same on each page. Maintenance is also

For individual use only—reproduction or duplication of this copyrighted material is prohibited.

Copyright Goodheart-Willcox Co., Inc.

simplified by having the same items on each page. When making a change to a user interface button, the designer would only need to upload one new image file and all the buttons referencing that file would be updated. Users also benefit from the reuse of buttons through improved usability of the website or user interface. The user would quickly learn the location of buttons and how the user interface works. Each new page or level would feel familiar. This adds to the user's understanding and navigation of the program. As an added benefit, reusing the same buttons or objects also reduces the overall file size and provides faster loading and shorter download times.

Lesson Review

Vocabulary

In a word processing document or on a sheet of paper, list all of the *key terms* in this lesson. Place each term on a separate line. Then, write a definition for each term using your own words. You will continue to build this terminology dictionary throughout this certification guide.

Review Questions

Answer the following questions. These questions are aligned to questions in the certification exam. Answering these questions will help prepare you to take the exam.

1. List the seven elements of art.

2. What are primitives?

3. From which colors are all colors on the color wheel created?

4. What is the difference between a complementary and an analogous color?

For individual use only—reproduction or duplication of this copyrighted material is prohibited.

5. What is the difference between positive space and negative space?

_____

_____

_____

_____

6. What is a vanishing point?

_____

_____

_____

_____

7. List the principles of design for most design projects.

_____

_____

_____

8. Which principle of design involves implied action for an object?

_____

9. Which principle of design involves drawing attention to an object by making it brighter, larger, or moving?

_____

10. Which principle of design is demonstrated by the images below?

_____

Pixel Embargo/Shutterstock.com; kaband/Shutterstock.com

11. Describe how the rule of thirds helps alignment of elements in a scene or image.

_____

_____

_____

_____

For individual use only—reproduction or duplication of this copyrighted material is prohibited.   Copyright Goodheart-Willcox Co., Inc.

12. Which principle of design describes why a blue object is hard to see on a blue background?

_____

13. Which principle of design involves making all the parts of a scene work together?

_____

14. Why would a designer copy and paste the same button design on all web pages on a website?

_____
_____
_____
_____

15. What are three benefits of maintaining unity of design?

_____
_____
_____
_____
_____
_____

 For individual use only—reproduction or duplication of this copyrighted material is prohibited.

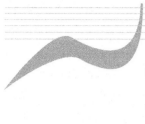

Lesson 2
Color Models, Images, and Fonts

Objectives

Students will describe common color models. Students will classify images as raster or vector. Students will discuss sizing and resolution of digital images. Students will identify serif and sans serif fonts.

Color Models

Colors are defined using a *color model,* which is a way of mixing base colors to create a spectrum of colors. The RGB and CMYK color models are the most common color models used in graphic design. The name of the *RGB* color model comes from the three base colors used in the color model: red, green, and blue. All of the colors you see on a computer screen are made by mixing these three base colors. The name of the *CMYK* color model comes from the process colors used in commercial printing: cyan, magenta, and yellow. K stands for key color. The most detail in a printed image appears in the key color, which is almost always black. Other color models include hue, saturation, luminescence (HSL); hexadecimal; and L*A*B* color, as shown in **Figure 2-1.**

The *hue, saturation, and luminescence (HSL)* color model, also known as the hue, saturation, and brightness (HSB) color model, creates color by adjusting these elements. Hue is the pigment color, saturation is how dark or rich the color is, and luminescence or brightness is how much light is shining on the color. This model is popular in creating textures and surfaces for 3D models. Since 3D models require the use of light and shadow to define position relative to the light source, using this color model allows the computer to leave the hue and saturation of the texture unchanged while adjusting the luminescence setting to be brighter on the surface facing the light source and darker on the surface facing away from the light source.

Hexadecimal color model is an RGB color model in which colors are represented by a series of six letters and numbers. This color model is used in web page design. Many imaging software programs allow the user to limit colors to "web only," which are 216 colors universally compatible with web browsers.

The *L*A*B** color model seeks to create natural colors as the human eye would see them. The description of the L*A*B* color model is a bit complicated as the L is for lightness and the A and B components are derived from a nonlinear color matrix, similar to an X,Y coordinate graph. Additionally, L*A*B* color model is used to convert RGB color models to CMYK color models or vice versa. L*A*B* color works for both video displays (RGB) and printed materials (CMYK) and is considered device independent.

For individual use only—reproduction or duplication of this copyrighted material is prohibited.

Color Model	Features	Method
HSL (also known as HSB or HSV)	Creates color by a combination of hue, saturation, and luminescence (or brightness or value). This model is popular in creating textures and surfaces for 3D models. Since 3D models require the use of light and shadow to define position relative to the light source in the game, using this color model allows the computer to leave the hue and saturation of the texture unchanged while adjusting the luminescence setting to be brighter on the surface facing the light source and darker on the surface facing away from the light source.	Additive
RGB	Creates color by a combination of red, green, and blue. Blending these three colors allows for over 16 million colors at 8-bit depth.	Additive
RGBA	The RGB color model with support for alpha channels. Alpha channels are transparency channels. The alpha channel sets the saturation of an RGB color from full opacity (not see-through) to full transparency (completely see-through).	Additive
Hexadecimal	An RGB color model in which the color is represented as a series of six letters and numbers. This color model is used in web page design. Many imaging software programs allow the user to limit colors to "web only," which are 216 colors universally compatible with web browsers.	Additive
CMYK	Creates color by a combination of cyan, magenta, yellow, and a key color that is almost always black. This model is used for printed materials. Each of the colors corresponds to one of the four printing plates on a printing press.	Subtractive
L*A*B*	The description of the L*A*B* color model is a bit complicated as the L is for lightness and the A and B components are derived from a nonlinear color matrix, similar to an X,Y coordinate graph. This model seeks to create natural-looking colors. Additionally, L*A*B* color model is used to convert RGB color models to CMYK color models or vice versa. L*A*B* color works for both video displays (RGB) and printed materials (CMYK) and is considered device independent.	Matrix of both additive and subtractive combinations

Goodheart-Willcox Publisher

Figure 2-1.

A comparison of common color models.

The total spectrum of colors a given model can create is called the *gamut.* Colors are assembled or blended using an additive or subtractive method. The *additive method* starts with no color, or black, and colors are added to create the final color. White in an additive color model is the combination of all color wavelengths in light. In the RGB color model, black is red 0, green 0, and blue 0. This means no color is added to the black screen. White is red 255, green 255, and blue 255. This means the maximum amount of all three colors is added to the black screen.

The *subtractive method* starts with all color, or white, and colors are removed to create the final color. For example, when you look at a red object, all color wavelengths in the light are absorbed by the paint (subtracted) except for red. What you see is the red wavelength. White is the reflection of all color wavelengths, so no color is subtracted. Black occurs when no color wavelengths are reflected, so all color is subtracted. CMYK is a subtractive color model. Black is cyan 100%, magenta 100%, yellow 100%, and key 100%. White is cyan 0%, magenta 0%, yellow 0%, and key 0%.

Copyright Goodheart-Willcox Co., Inc.   For individual use only—reproduction or duplication of this copyrighted material is prohibited.

Images

There are two basic types of images: raster and vector. All images created using a computer fall into one of these two categories. Additionally, digital images may be compressed to save storage space and reduce transmission times.

Raster Images

Raster images are images that are made of dots or pixels. Each pixel in the image has a specific color and location to construct the final image. A raster image is called a *bitmap* because the location and color of each pixel is mapped. The computer reads a bitmap image by creating a coordinate grid with the origin at the top-left corner and increasing the X value moving right and the Y value moving down. In each space of the coordinate grid is a single pixel. A pixel can only be one color. To determine the color of a pixel at a particular coordinate location, the color value of a pixel is read by the computer and displayed.

Originally, bitmaps were only made at a bit depth of 1. *Bit depth* is a binary measurement for color. Binary allows for only two values, either a 1 or a 0. A bit depth of 1 describes the exponent value of the binary digit. A bit depth of 1 means 2^1. A bitmap value of 1 would, therefore, assign a white pixel on the coordinate grid where required. This produces a black and white image with no gray.

Eventually, computers were able to read bitmaps to a bit depth of 4. A bit depth of 4 allowed for a total of 16 colors, as 2^4 equals 16. The modern minimum standard for computer-displayed color is a bit depth of 8 or higher. A bit depth of 8, or 2^8, allows for 256 colors. Two hundred fifty-six–color devices are typically handheld devices where graphic quality is not needed. Computer monitors, HDTVs, and other devices that require quality graphics try to achieve true color or deep color.

True color has a bit depth of 24. True color uses the familiar RGB color model with 256 shades of red, 256 shades of green, and 256 shades of blue. True color produces 2^{24} colors, or 16,777,216 colors. Since the human eye is only capable of discriminating a little more than 10 million colors, 24-bit color can result in more colors than the human eye can see. Other color depths above 24 bit fall into the deep color range. *Deep color* is supported by Windows 7 and later up to a 48-bit depth. This provides more intense colors and shadow. Deep color can produce a gamut of over 1 billion colors.

Bit depth also allows for transparency. With a large gamut of color, an alpha channel can be allocated. The *alpha channel* varies the opacity of the color. The alpha channel can support from full transparency all the way to full opacity. A 16-bit alpha channel can support 65,536 values of transparency.

Alpha channels can also allow for a masking color. A *masking color* is a single shade of a color that can be set to be transparent. If you have ever seen a weather report on TV, you have likely seen a masking color in use. Using a green or blue screen, called a chroma screen, will allow a background of the weather map to digitally replace the blank screen. In image creation, mask colors are typically chosen so they will not interfere with natural colors. Using a masking color such as white would be a very bad choice. If white were made to be transparent, then the white in a person's eyes and other white items would be transparent.

For individual use only—reproduction or duplication of this copyrighted material is prohibited.   Copyright Goodheart-Willcox Co., Inc.

Vector Images

Vector images are images composed of lines, curves, and fills. Vector images do not store the color value and location of each pixel. Rather, the image is displayed based on the mathematical definition of each element in the image. In other words, in a raster image a line is composed of dots, while in a vector image the line is defined by a mathematical equation. For a vector image to be displayed, the software must rasterize the image before it is sent to the display device.

Some software programs can also convert raster images into vector images. This process is called *bitmap tracing.* The software will trace around zones that are the same or similar color to create a closed region and fill the region with a color.

A vector image can be a very small file size because the image is drawn by the computer using a mathematical formula. Since the formula draws the image, the image can be resized infinitely smaller or larger without loss of clarity, as shown in **Figure 2-2.** This is one of the biggest advantages of a vector image.

However, raster images offer an advantage over vector images because a vector image requires the CPU to work hard to draw the image. In the world of handheld devices with small CPUs and low memory, a vector image may have the benefit of a small file size, but may take up a large amount of CPU ability. Bitmaps do not take up a large amount of CPU ability, but have higher file size. The designer will need

Goodheart-Willcox Publisher; image: Andreas Meyer/Shutterstock.com

Figure 2-2.

Raster images become pixelated when enlarged, but vector images can be infinitely scaled.

Copyright Goodheart-Willcox Co., Inc.   For individual use only—reproduction or duplication of this copyrighted material is prohibited.

to understand the limits and capabilities of each device on which the image will be rendered to correctly match the file size and CPU usage to prevent lag and crashing the device.

Image File Compression

When working with images that are used on web pages or mobile devices, a designer should optimize the images. *Optimizing* an image is applying the most appropriate resolution and image file compression to achieve the smallest file size for the image quality needed. *Compression* uses mathematical formulas to approximate the location and color of each pixel and thereby reduce the total file size. Raster images are often compressed from their original raw format to reduce file size, save computer memory, and decrease download time.

A computer algorithm is used to record the pixel data in a smaller file size and then uncompress the image when it is opened in image-editing software. Almost all compression formats seek to eliminate the color values stored in the image that are beyond the capability of the human eye. The two most popular image-compression algorithms are lossy and lossless. The *lossy compression algorithm* compresses the image, but does not keep perfect image clarity. The image generally will have an acceptable appearance, but it will not be as clear when uncompressed as the original image. The *lossless compression algorithm,* or losslessly compression algorithm, compresses the image and keeps perfect clarity when uncompressed. There is a tradeoff between clarity and file size. To reduce the file size to run on a handheld device, the clarity may need to be reduced to fit the memory needs of the device and program.

File formats are needed for each type of compression so the computer will understand how to read the compressed image. **Figure 2-3** lists several popular image file formats and the compression model needed to expand the image.

Image Sizing and Resolution

When a bitmap image is enlarged, the existing pixels spread out. This *dithers* the image, which creates holes in the image where the pixels are no longer touching each other. Dithering can also occur when color is undefined in the program such as a web browser. Software uses a process called interpolation to dither an image. *Interpolation* is the refining of the space between pixels. During interpolation, the software averages the color of all pixels touching the empty space. The average color of the surrounding pixels is then assigned to the new pixel.

Part of optimizing a raster image is setting the proper resolution for the intended output. For example, an app for the iPad should have an icon that is 144 pixels × 144 pixels so the icon will properly display on the device and in the app store. A standard computer monitor has a resolution of 72 dots per inch (dpi) or 96 dpi. Making images for a website with a resolution higher than 96 dpi would not be properly optimizing the images. On the other hand, most images for print publication should be sized to specific dimensions with a resolution of 300 dpi.

For individual use only—reproduction or duplication of this copyrighted material is prohibited.

File Format	Name	Image Type	Compression	Benefit
GIF	Graphic Interface Format	Raster	Lossless	Popular for use on websites; 256 colors and can be animated
PNG-8	Portable Network Graphic, 8-bit depth	Raster	Lossless	Same as GIF, but cannot be animated
PNG-24	Portable Network Graphic, 24-bit depth	Raster	Lossless	Same as PNG-8, but millions of colors and transparency options
JPEG	Joint Photographic Expert Group	Raster	Lossy	Generally offers the smallest file size
BMP	Bitmap	Raster	Run length encoded (RLE)	Device independent
RAW or CIFF	Camera Image File Format	Raster	None	Raw data at full uncompressed value obtained from a digital camera or scanner
CGM	Computer Graphics Metafile	Vector	Vector	Can be used with many vector-imaging programs
AI	Adobe Illustrator	Vector	Vector	For use with Adobe Illustrator
EPS	Encapsulated PostScript	Vector	Vector	Generic vector format that can be used in any PostScript-enabled software

Goodheart-Willcox Publisher

Figure 2-3.
Common file formats for graphics.

The resolution of an image is measured in *dots per inch (dpi)* or *pixels per inch (ppi)*. This measure is the number of dots or pixels along the horizontal axis of an image multiplied by the number of dots or pixels along the vertical axis of the image. An image that is one inch square with 200 pixels on each axis has horizontal and vertical resolutions of 200 dpi. If this image is stretched to two inches square without resampling, the resolution becomes 100 dpi, which results in a loss of image clarity. If an image with a horizontal resolution of 200 dpi is 5 inches wide, the horizontal dimension contains 1000 pixels (5 inches × 200 dpi = 1000 pixels).

When an image is resized, it must be *resampled* to create a new image without reducing the image resolution. Resampling interpolates the image, adding or removing pixels as needed. Most imaging software gives the designer options for selecting a resampling method. A common resampling method is bicubic. There are two variations of bicubic resampling: bicubic for reduction and bicubic for enlargement. *Bicubic for reduction* is optimized for removing pixels, while *bicubic for enlargement* is optimized for creating pixels.

Fonts

A *font*, or *typeface*, is a collection of letters, numbers, and symbols that are all of the same design or style. The font can be important in conveying meaning in a design project. Text set in one font may communicate elegance, while the same text set in a different font may communicate excitement or tension.

The two basic designs of font or typeface are serif and sans serif. *Serifs* are decorative marks at the ends of letters, as shown in **Figure 2-4.** The word *sans*

Copyright Goodheart-Willcox Co., Inc.   For individual use only—reproduction or duplication of this copyrighted material is prohibited.

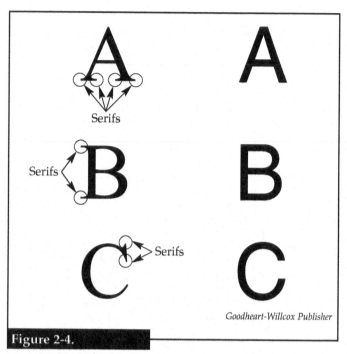

Goodheart-Willcox Publisher

Figure 2-4.

A comparison of serif and sans serif typefaces.

means without, so *sans serif* means without serif. There is much debate over which is more readable. Traditionally, serif type is used for long passages where readability is important, such as books, while sans serif type is used when legibility is important, such as street signs. However, there is no clear agreement among experts as to the significance between serif and sans serif type when it comes to readability and legibility. It is generally thought that a sans serif typeface promotes the feeling of security, trust, and strength, which is why this type is typically used in logos and headlines.

Other typefaces that fall outside of serif or sans serif classification include novelty, ornate, handwritten, script, and ornamental. These are used as decoration or as an attention item on a page and should not be used when creating the body text. In addition to being hard to read, they may have the added problem of not being installed on the user's computer, which is important in web page design. If a device does not have a specified font, whether decorative, serif, or sans serif, it will be displayed in a substitute font.

Lesson Review

Vocabulary

In a word processing document or on a sheet of paper, list all of the **key terms** in this lesson. Place each term on a separate line. Then, write a definition for each term using your own words. You will continue to build this terminology dictionary throughout this certification guide.

Review Questions

Answer the following questions. These questions are aligned to questions in the certification exam. Answering these questions will help prepare you to take the exam.

1. Which raster image file type supports millions of colors and transparency?

_____

2. List six common raster image file types.

_____

_____

_____

_____

For individual use only—reproduction or duplication of this copyrighted material is prohibited.

3. List three common vector image file types.

_____

_____

4. Which color model and resolution (in dpi) would be best for an image used on a website that is viewed from a desktop computer?

_____

5. Describe how an alpha channel and masking color control image transparency.

_____

_____

_____

_____

6. Which type of image is composed of lines, curves, and fills?

_____

7. Describe bitmap tracing.

_____

_____

_____

_____

8. Compare and contrast raster images with vector images.

_____

_____

_____

_____

9. What are the two aspects of optimizing a raster image for use on a website or handheld device?

_____

_____

_____

_____

10. How can an uncompressed RAW image file type be obtained?

_____

_____

11. Explain what happens when an image contains a color that is undefined in a web browser.

_____

_____

_____

Copyright Goodheart-Willcox Co., Inc.   For individual use only—reproduction or duplication of this copyrighted material is prohibited.

12. If the resolution of an image is 72 dpi and the image is 8 inches wide by 10 inches tall, how many pixels wide is the image?

_____

13. Which bicubic resampling method is best if enlarging an image from 300 pixels wide to 800 pixels wide?

_____

14. Describe the difference between a serif and sans serif font.

_____

_____

_____

_____

15. Which font design is generally thought to instill trust in the reader?

_____

For individual use only—reproduction or duplication of this copyrighted material is prohibited.

Copyright Goodheart-Willcox Co., Inc.

Lesson 3 Digital-Project Management

Objectives

Students will evaluate the preproduction stage of production for a digital media project. Students will describe conversion of traditional artwork and photographs into digital assets. Students will compare and contrast hard and soft proofs. Students will discuss collaboration and sharing of assets.

Reading Materials

A program such as Adobe Illustrator allows the designer to use different digital brushes and tools to create artwork. A *digital brush* is used by the artist to produce effects similar to a traditional paintbrush, except the effects are virtual, being created in the computer software. The designer uses the software to set a brush shape and a color to paint with, and then uses an input device to create the artwork.

An *input device* is a piece of computer equipment that takes information from the user, such as hand movement, and translates it into signals the computer and software program can use. The keyboard and mouse are standard input devices found on most desktop computers, while tablets have a touch-screen display used for input. Digital artists often use a dedicated drawing tablet or a pressure-sensitive touch-screen device to create digital artwork. A drawing tablet is shown in **Figure 3-1.**

Andrey_Popov/Shutterstock.com

Figure 3-1.

Many professional illustrators use a drawing tablet as an input device for creating artwork.

The digital brushes in illustration programs are not limited to a single effect, as is the case with traditional paint brushes. A digital brush can also paint using patterns and styles that only exist as digital tools. The *vector brush library* in Adobe Illustrator contains many different types of brushes that can be used to paint patterns. As you learn to use Illustrator, you will be able to use digital brushes and tools to create impressive digital art.

A digital artist must know more than just the software functions. The most valuable employees can take control of a design project and create a finished work to the client's expectations. As a digital artist, you will be fully responsible for creating sample graphics and the final image of the project. Working with the client throughout the stages of production will allow you to narrow your focus on producing the best graphics for the job.

Copyright Goodheart-Willcox Co., Inc.   For individual use only—reproduction or duplication of this copyrighted material is prohibited.

A design project will follow a path through the four stages of production. These stages, in order, are: preproduction, production, testing, and publication. The *preproduction stage* includes client interviews, analysis of the target market, and creating sketches or storyboards to summarize planning and analysis. In the *production stage*, sketches are refined, the design is finalized, and the product is created. During the *testing stage*, the performance of the product is tested on technology devices that will be used by the target market. Testing with subjects from the target market is also conducted to ensure the product aligns to the client's goals. The last stage, the *publication stage*, is when final revisions from testing results are implemented. After final revisions are complete, the product is published for public use.

Preproduction Stage

The preproduction stage is the most important stage of production. The preproduction stage involves gathering information and planning out how the job will get done. During preproduction, the project manager will interview the client, conduct research, and gather customer demographic information to best determine what project requirements need to be met. Afterward, the project manager is responsible for:

- selecting the best team members for the job;
- identifying the tasks; and
- determining deadlines for that project.

Preproduction Interviews

The *client* is the person requesting the work. When working with a client, it is important to have a full understanding of what he or she expects. You should conduct *preproduction interviews* with the client to brainstorm ideas and fully communicate the goals for the finished product. A preproduction interview occurs *before* any work begins. If you start working without this important step, the client may be dissatisfied with the result, and you would have to redo the project. In the professional world, you are paid by the client, and the client will not pay for unsatisfactory work that does not meet the specified goals. Working with the client in a preproduction interview, you will need to identify the client goals and target market. These are the two basic criteria that will guide the project.

The *client goals* set the direction of the creative work. The client is paying you to create something to meet a goal, often attracting customers. This means the graphics and layout need to meet these goals, or the client will feel he or she did not receive the service for which payment was made. Client goals can include what the graphics will be used for, such as packaging, website, billboard, employee handbook, etc., and the specifications for graphics. The specifications for an image used on a billboard will be much different than for an image used on a website. Additionally, the client may have goals of informing or attracting attention. The use of color is important in attracting attention, while color in information items may have little value.

The *target market* is a group of people for whom the work is intended. The target market for a cartoon-style image is likely very different from the target market for a photorealistic image. If the target market is children, an advertising project may have little or no text, may contain fantasy characters, and may use bright colors. If

For individual use only—reproduction or duplication of this copyrighted material is prohibited.

the audience is college graduates, the advertisement may contain large blocks of text and photorealistic images or photographs.

A target market is defined by its demographics. *Demographics* are shared traits of a group. The demographics of a high school class might include age, achievement, and geographic location. The students in a single 11th grade class might all be ages 15–17 years, passed the 10th grade, and live within three miles of the school. It is important to understand demographics because demographics help segment a population of people into smaller groups that have similar characteristics. The similarities allow the designer to create items that will appeal to that specific target audience and not everyone in the population.

Preproduction Deliverables and Communication

Before starting to build a project in Adobe Illustrator, preproduction deliverables should be defined and created. These should be communicated to the client along with any other information that is relevant to the project.

Preproduction deliverables include sketches and specifications. From the client interviews, you can work out the use of the images and find out the quality needed. *Sketching* the design is creating a freehand drawing of the design, which is always a great way to show the client that you understand what he or she wants and how to create the finished product. *Specifications* include the scope of the work to be done and the deadline. The *deadline* is the date the project must be delivered to the client.

Scope defines how the image will be output in final form and the intended use. Is the image going to go on a webpage, or is it going to be on a roadside billboard? The difference between these final forms greatly affects the way the digital design work is done. The documentation of a project's scope, which is called a *scope statement, scope of project document,* or *statement of work,* explains the boundaries of the project and establishes responsibilities for each team member. During the project, this documentation helps the team stay focused and on task. The scope statement also provides the team with guidelines for making decisions about requests for changes during the project.

Part of the scope is a definition of the formality of the project. *Formality* is the degree to which something follows an accepted set of rules. Events have varying degrees of formality. A wedding is often very formal—it has high formality— with an elaborate production of wedding gowns, tuxedos, limousines, and more. However, a wedding may be very informal—it has low formality—with just the bride and groom wearing flip-flops and swimsuits in a small ceremony at the beach. The designer of the wedding invitations for these weddings needs to know how formal or informal to make the design. Products such as restaurant menus need to match the formality of the location. Formality must match the client goals, purpose of the document, and the needs of the target market for the design to be effective.

Preproduction deliverables enhance the communication and understanding between the client and design team. The design team is responsible for keeping the client informed and part of the process throughout every stage of the design project. Use the following best practices to help achieve a successful relationship with the client.

- During preproduction, use sketches and mockups to help the client visualize the designs you are planning to create.
- To track the changes and approval of the client, make notes on the sketches and have the client approve the basic design by signing the sketches, which creates a record of the client's approval for any changes to the project.

Copyright Goodheart-Willcox Co., Inc.   For individual use only—reproduction or duplication of this copyrighted material is prohibited.

- Updating the client on the overall progress and getting approval on any completed artwork limits the chances of having problems at the end.

Before the preproduction phase ends, the designer should have a firm understanding of what the client wants and the design elements that need to be created.

Conversion of Traditional Artwork and Printed Photographs

The digital artist may need to perform a *conversion* to change physical art into a digital format, or to *digitize* the artwork. Typically, conversions are performed on traditional artwork such as drawings, paintings, and continuous tone (nondigital) photographs. When performing these conversions, the most important consideration is the technology needed to properly convert the image to the best quality of digital image for the application. A sketch may simply need to be photographed by a digital camera to make it a digital sketch. A digital camera takes a photograph, but in digital form instead of on film. A high-quality painting might need a digital scanner to capture the quality of the image. A digital scanner passes light over an image, similar to how a photocopy machine works, and digitally records each point of color. A digital camera or scanner creates a raster image when it records each point of color. Other items that may need to be converted into digital format are photographic slides or other nonstandard images. *Slides* are photographs printed on transparent film from which the image is projected onto a screen to view it. Special equipment is often needed to properly transfer slides to digital format.

Whenever possible, have the client submit the images in digital format so you do not have to do the conversions. This will save you time and also place the responsibility for the quality of the conversion on the client. The client can also save money by not having to pay you to do the conversions. However, in many cases the client will not have the ability to do the conversion or the technical knowledge to provide the proper quality.

Proofs

Before creating the final images in all the required formats, the client should review and approve the work. The output you provide the client is a proof. A *proof* is a copy of the final output created for approval. When client signs off on a proof, he or she is giving approval to create the final output needed. A *hard proof* is a physical proof printed on paper or various other substrates, while a *soft proof* is viewed on the computer. You may also want to use Adobe Illustrator to do a soft proof preview. Illustrator offers a soft-proof mode to simulate how a printed image will be rendered when output. Using the Working CMYK proof setup in Illustrator converts the printable CMYK color model into the video RGB color model displayed on the computer monitor. This is the default viewing mode in Illustrator.

An advantage of a soft proof or electronic proof over a hard proof is the ability to quickly see how the image would look in different outputs. Changing color models or output devices will change the overall look of the image in the soft proof. To do the same thing with a hard proof, a new proof would have to be pulled for each version. Soft proofs are also a cost-saving device, as hard proofs can be expensive to generate.

For individual use only—reproduction or duplication of this copyrighted material is prohibited.   Copyright Goodheart-Willcox Co., Inc.

Collaboration and Sharing Assets

Many times you will be collaborating with other designers during a project. Using the Adobe Creative Cloud, CS Review, and Adobe Bridge will help organize and share work. *Adobe Creative Cloud* offers a way to share files, give feedback, and save settings across devices. *CS Review* allows others to review your work without sharing the original source file. *Adobe Bridge* or, in CS6, the **Mini Bridge** tab, provides a convenient portal to store design elements, such as images, used in more than one Adobe program. For example, an image altered in Adobe Illustrator will be used in Adobe Dreamweaver to create a website. Adobe Bridge allows the image to be placed in the Dreamweaver web page. The Illustrator artist can later manipulate the image and save it in Adobe Bridge. The image will automatically update in the Dreamweaver web page. Adobe Bridge provides a convenient way to manage, open, and view design assets and files.

Adobe Bridge allows an image file to be linked from one program to another. *Linking* maintains a connection to the original image file. If the image file is updated in the source program, it is automatically updated in the shared program. If the image is *embedded*, however, it is a copy of the image without a connection to the original file. Altering the original image file does not automatically update the image in the shared program. In order to update the image in the shared program, the existing image must be manually replaced with the updated image.

Lesson Review

Vocabulary

In a word processing document or on a sheet of paper, list all of the *key terms* in this lesson. Place each term on a separate line. Then, write a definition for each term using your own words. You will continue to build this terminology dictionary throughout this certification guide.

Review Questions

Answer the following questions. These questions are aligned to questions in the certification exam. Answering these questions will help prepare you to take the exam.

1. List the four stages of the project development process in the correct order.

_____

_____

_____

_____

2. What are three responsibilities of a project manager during preproduction?

_____

_____

_____

_____

For individual use only—reproduction or duplication of this copyrighted material is prohibited.

3. What two criteria should guide the digital artist when creating art for a client?

_____

_____

_____

4. What are three techniques that may be used in creating an advertisement for children?

_____

_____

_____

_____

5. Why does a designer need to understand the demographics of the target audience?

_____

_____

_____

_____

6. Which level of formality would you expect a menu from a drive-through restaurant to have? Explain your answer using specific details that support your claim.

_____

_____

_____

_____

_____

7. Images produced with a scanner or digital camera are which type of image? Why?

_____

_____

_____

_____

8. Which Illustrator setup is best for viewing artwork on a computer monitor for a brochure that will be printed?

_____

For individual use only—reproduction or duplication of this copyrighted material is prohibited.

9. Which three features in Adobe Illustrator allow sharing of art assets between other Adobe programs?

_____

_____

_____

_____

_____

10. What is the difference between a linked image and an embedded image?

_____

_____

_____

_____

Copyright Goodheart-Willcox Co., Inc.   For individual use only—reproduction or duplication of this copyrighted material is prohibited.

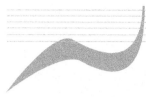

Lesson 4
Illustrator Interface

Objectives

Students will describe a workspace. Students will use Illustrator tools. Students will explain the function of layers. Students will apply various colors to Illustrator shapes. Students will use a panel menu. Students will discuss the use of smart guides. Students will evaluate color according to harmony rules. Students will modify pattern swatches. Students will manage artboards on the canvas. Students will use rulers and the grid. Students will create new shapes from multiple individual shapes. Students will apply a blend between shapes. Students will describe how to create a customized workspace. Students will export artboards to a PSD file.

Situation

The Nocturnal Interactive Computer Entertainment (NICE) company is hiring a new apprentice for its digital image department. You have interviewed for the job and have been given a chance to participate in the apprentice program. To be hired as a full-time artist with the company, you will have to pass the Adobe Certified Associate (ACA) Illustrator Creative Cloud industry certification exam. The first step in preparing for the exam is to gain experience using the functions of the software.

How to Begin

TIP
Adobe Creative Cloud provides running updates of the software. As a result, the version of the software you are using may be slightly different than the screen captures and tools illustrated in this certification guide.

TIP
The [Ctrl][N] key combination can be used to quickly display the **New Document** dialog box.

1. Before beginning this lesson, download the needed files from the student companion website located at www.g-wlearning.com, and unzip them into your working folder.

2. Launch Adobe Illustrator Creative Cloud.

3. If a splash page or quick launch window appears, click the close button (**X**) in the top-right corner of the window to close it.

4. Click the **File** pull-down menu on the menu bar at the top of the screen, and click **New...** in the menu (**File>New...**). The **New Document** dialog box is displayed, as shown in **Figure 4-1.**

5. Enter *LastName*_Circles in the **Name:** text box. This is the name of the artwork, which will be the default file name when the file is saved for the first time.

6. Click the **Profile:** drop-down arrow, and click **Web** in the drop-down list. This is a preset profile that creates a single artboard in RGB color model. Notice that many of the other settings in the dialog box are automatically changed. A preset profile contains various default settings that are typically appropriate for a given type of project.

7. Click the **Portrait** button in the **Orientation:** area so it is on (depressed or shaded). The orientation is the direction the paper is turned and can be set to

For individual use only—reproduction or duplication of this copyrighted material is prohibited.

Copyright Goodheart-Willcox Co., Inc.

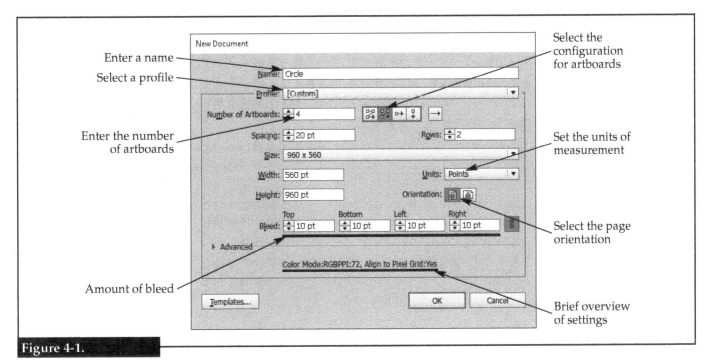

Figure 4-1.

Creating a new Adobe Illustrator document.

either portrait or landscape. *Portrait* orientation has the short end of the paper at the top and bottom like a sheet of notebook paper. *Landscape* orientation has the short end of the paper at the left and right like a flat-screen television. Also notice that the preset profile has changed to Custom. A *custom profile* is any document profile that does not exactly match a preset option. Even if you change the orientation back to landscape, the profile will still be Custom.

8. In the **Bleed:** area, enter 10 px (ten pixels) in the **Top** text box. By default, the values in the **Top**, **Bottom**, **Left**, and **Right** text boxes are locked, as indicated by the button to the right of the text boxes, so 10 px is automatically entered in the three other text boxes. The *bleed* is the distance beyond the final trimmed edge of the printed sheet where the image can extend. When the sheet is trimmed to final size, the portion of the image in the bleed is trimmed off. This ensures the color (image) extends to the very edge of the paper. The bleed is needed to compensate for normal variations in the equipment used to trim the sheets to final size.

9. Click the **Units:** drop-down arrow, and click **Points** in the drop-down list. *Point* is a unit of measurement used in the printing, publishing, and graphic design industries. One point is equal to 1/72 of an inch. Notice that when this setting is changed to points, the units in the **Bleed:** text boxes automatically change to points (pt) as well, but the values themselves do not change.

10. Enter 4 in the **Number of Artboards:** text box. An *artboard* is where the images you create will be placed. These are like sheets of paper. There can be more than one artboard for a document. All of the artboards in a document are placed on the canvas. The *canvas* is a like a large table that holds all the sheets of paper. You can also draw on the canvas, but anything on the canvas will not be output to the final image. Only the content of an artboard can be saved as an image or printed.

11. Click the **Grid by Column** button to the right of the **Number of Artboards:** text box. This will arrange the four artboards in columns on the canvas. The name of the button can be displayed in help text by hovering the cursor over the button. To *hover* means to place the cursor over an item without clicking or moving.

TIP
To return to the settings of the preset profile, reselect the profile in the **Profile:** drop-down list.

TIP
If you will be working in the printing, publishing, or graphic design industries, it is important to learn to think of distances in terms of points and picas. There are 72 points in one inch. There are 12 points in one pica, and six picas in one inch.

Copyright Goodheart-Willcox Co., Inc.   For individual use only—reproduction or duplication of this copyrighted material is prohibited.

12. Click the **OK** button to close the dialog box and start the new document. Notice that the document name appears in the tab above the canvas, as shown in **Figure 4-2.** However, the file has not yet been saved.

13. Click **File>Save**. Since the file has not yet been saved, the **Save As** dialog box is displayed, which is a standard save-type dialog box.

14. Navigate to your working folder.

15. Verify the default file name in the **File name:** text box is *LastName*_Circles. Since the document was named when it was launched, that name should appear here. If not, enter the name.

16. Click the **Save as type:** drop-down arrow, and examine the different file formats in which the file can be saved. Click **Adobe Illustrator (*.AI)** in the list. The AI file type is the native format for Adobe Illustrator.

17. Click the **Save** button. The **Illustrator Options** dialog box is displayed, as shown in **Figure 4-3.** Settings for the file can be configured in this dialog box, as you will see in later lessons.

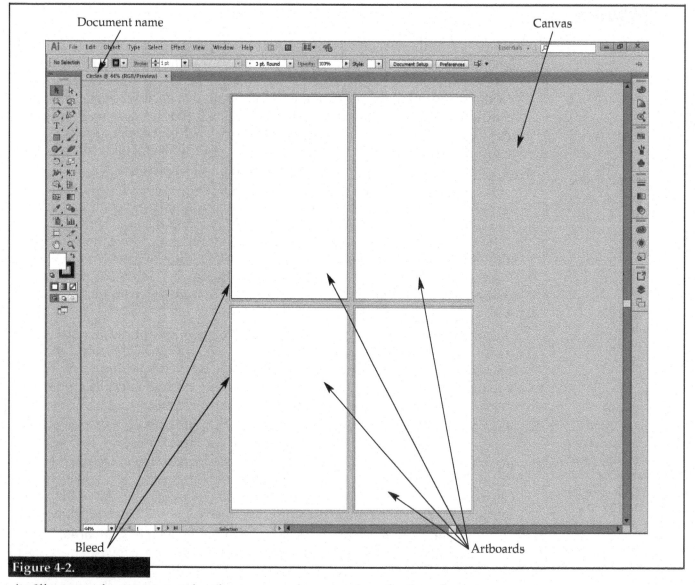

Document name   Canvas

Bleed   Artboards

Figure 4-2.

An Illustrator document contains the canvas and any number of artboards.

For individual use only—reproduction or duplication of this copyrighted material is prohibited.   Copyright Goodheart-Willcox Co., Inc.

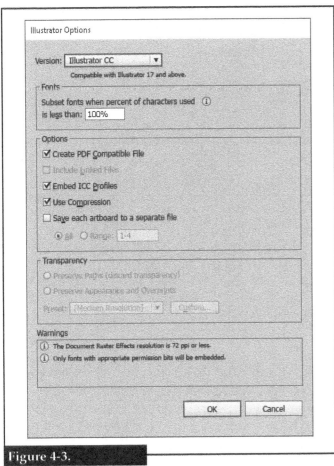

Figure 4-3.

When saving an Illustrator document for the first time, certain options must be set. In many cases, the default settings can be accepted.

18. Click the **OK** button to accept the default options and save the file. Notice that the .ai file extension is added to the document name in the tab above the canvas.

Workspace

A *workspace* is the layout of the toolbars, panels, and document on the screen. Several standardized workspaces are available in Illustrator, including workspaces such as Painting and Typography. You may also create custom views by dragging the workspace tools to different locations and saving the workspace. Changing the layout by moving panels, adding more tools, rearranging panels, or otherwise changing the screen setup changes the workspace.

Review the location and name for each tool shown in **Figure 4-4.** These will be referred to by name throughout these lessons. Note: the color scheme shown in the screen captures in this guide has been changed to a lighter scheme for easy viewing. The **Application** bar holds commands in a pull-down menu format. Click a pull-down menu to see the commands it contains, and then click a command to activate it. This bar also contains the workspace switcher.

The **Control** panel contains some basic tools and a contextual toolbar. A contextual toolbar, panel, or menu contains options or features for the active tool or selected shape. For example, if a line segment is selected, the **Control** panel displays settings for color, alignment, shapes, and transforms near the right-hand side of the bar.

The **Tools** panel holds the common tools used to design in Illustrator. Tools are organized on the panel by function with a line separating each group.

Illustrator makes use of panels. A panel is a small window that holds commands or options. A panel may be in a group by command function. A designer can arrange the panels in any configuration. The panels can even be moved from one panel group to another. Panels may be expanded with the commands visible or collapsed. Collapsed panels have been minimized to icons to save space on the screen. Clicking a panel icon will expand the panel.

The document tab displays the name of the document as well as the zoom percentage and the color space. The designer can have multiple documents open in Illustrator at the same time. Each document will have a separate document tab. The designer can navigate between open documents by simply clicking the different document tabs. Dragging a document tab off the document tab area opens the document in a separate window.

An *artboard* is the area where the images and scenes are created. It is like a page in a sketchbook. Here the artist can draw and color the scene. The area outside of the artboard is called the canvas. The *canvas* does not print and is not included

Copyright Goodheart-Willcox Co., Inc.   For individual use only—reproduction or duplication of this copyrighted material is prohibited.

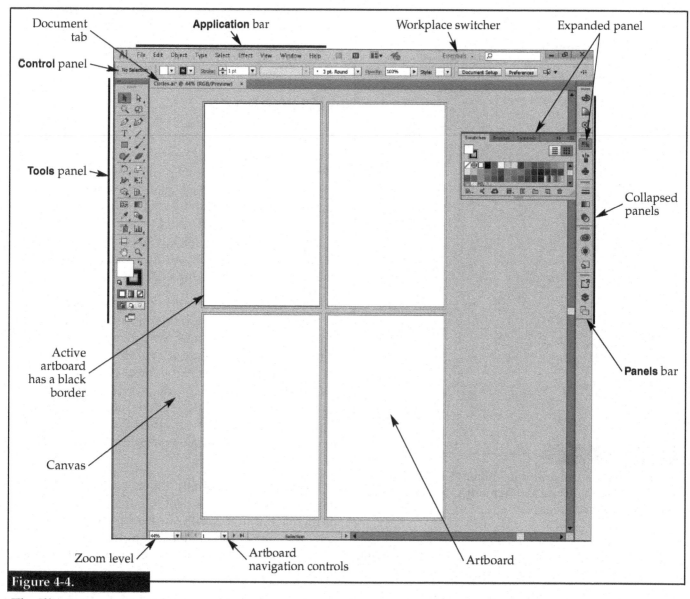

Figure 4-4.

The Illustrator user interface.

in exported images. Often, an artist will place items on the canvas so they can be combined and layered to create composite images. Those images can then be used in the scene on the artboard. Alternatively, the artist could create the composite image on a different artboard and move it where needed within the scene.

19. Locate the workspace switcher in the top-right corner of the screen, and click it to display a drop-down menu. Notice the standardized workspaces that are available, as shown in **Figure 4-5.** The current workspace is checked.

20. Click **Essentials** in the drop-down menu. This restores the Essentials workspace.

21. Click the bar at the top of the **Tools** panel, hold, and drag the panel to the middle of the screen. This panel is now *floating,* whereas before it was *docked.*

Color

22. Click the **Color** button in the **Panel** bar on the right side of the screen. This panel changes from *collapsed* to *expanded,* as shown in **Figure 4-6.** Notice that two other panels—**Color Guide** and **Color Themes**—are nested in the expanded panel along with the **Color** panel. Clicking the name of either panel brings that panel to the front.

For individual use only—reproduction or duplication of this copyrighted material is prohibited.   Copyright Goodheart-Willcox Co., Inc.

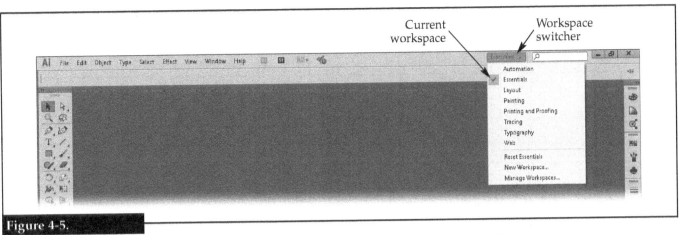

Figure 4-5.

There are a number of default workspaces that can be used to create drawings in Illustrator.

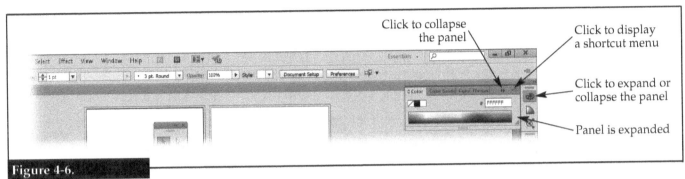

Figure 4-6.

The **Panel** bar contains collapsed panels that can be expanded. The **Panel** bar and the **Tools** panel are the two main means of accessing tools in Illustrator.

TIP

An expanded panel can be collapsed by clicking the button used to expand it. For example, to collapse the **Color** panel, click the **Color** button.

23. Click the double-chevron button (**>>**) in the top-right corner of the **Color** panel. This collapses the panel.

24. Click the workspace switcher, and click **Reset 'Essentials'** in the drop-down menu. This returns the Essentials workspace to the default settings. The changes you make are automatically saved to the current workspace, and resetting the workspace basically undoes those changes.

Tools

The Illustrator **Tools** panel contains buttons for various tools, which are organized in groups. Some tools have similar tools hidden under the tool shown by the button. A black triangle at the bottom-right corner of a button indicates that clicking the button will display a flyout. A *flyout* is a hidden toolbar that will "fly out" and be displayed like a panel. Clicking and holding a flyout button displays the flyout from which additional tools can be selected. A single click on the button will activate the tool displayed by the button without displaying the flyout.

25. Identify each of the tools shown in **Figure 4-7.** Hover the cursor over each tool in the **Tools** panel to display the name, and record the name of each tool in the figure. In some cases, you will need to click and hold the button to display the flyout in order to see the tool.

26. Identify each of the tools shown in **Figure 4-8.** Hover the cursor over each tool in the **Panels** bar to display the name, and record the name of each tool in the figure.

	Icon	Name		Icon	Name
1.	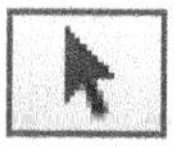		20.	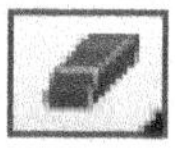	
2.	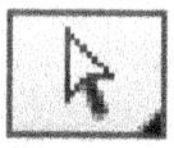		21.	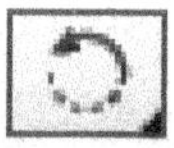	
3.	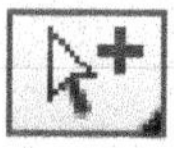		22.	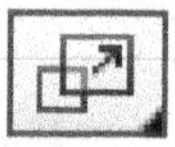	
4.	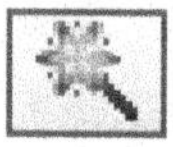		23.	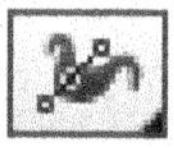	
5.	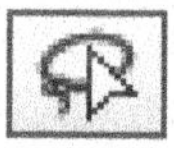		24.	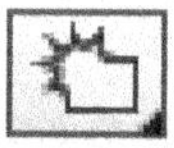	
6.	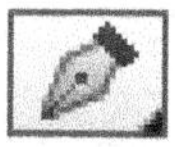		25.	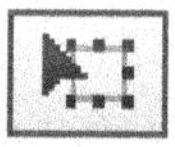	
7.	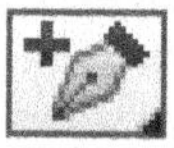		26.	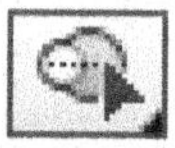	
8.	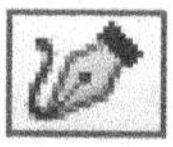		27.	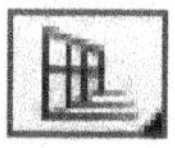	
9.	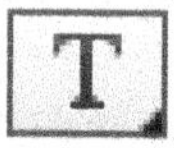		28.	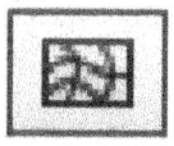	
10.	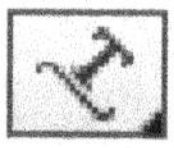		29.	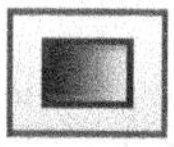	
11.	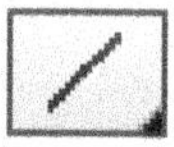		30.	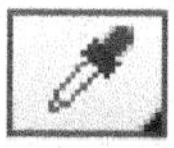	
12.	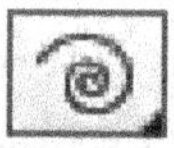		31.	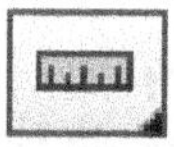	
13.	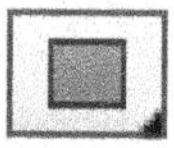		32.	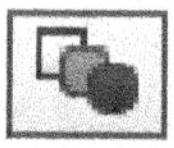	
14.	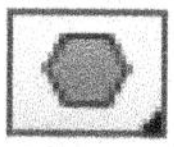		33.	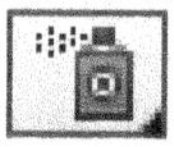	
15.	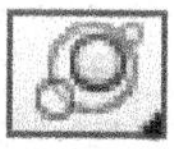		34.	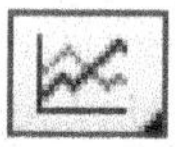	
16.	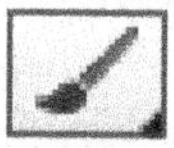		35.	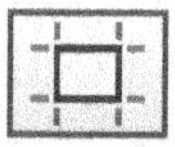	
17.	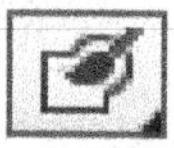		36.	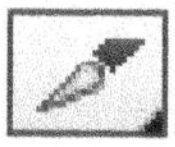	
18.	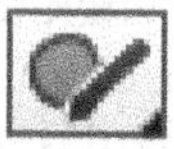		37.	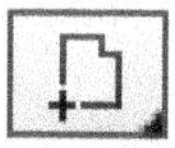	
19.	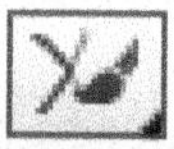		38.	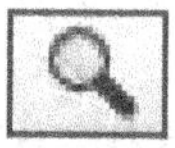	

Figure 4-7.

Write the name of each tool identified here.

For individual use only—reproduction or duplication of this copyrighted material is prohibited.

Copyright Goodheart-Willcox Co., Inc.

	Icon	Name		Icon	Name
1.			9.		
2.			10.		
3.			11.		
4.			12.		
5.			13.		
6.			14.		
7.			15.		
8.					

Figure 4-8.

Write the name of each tool identified here.

Rectangle Tool

27. Click the **Rectangle Tool** button in the **Tools** panel. The tool is activated, and the cursor changes to a crosshair or plus sign.

28. Click anywhere on the top-left artboard, hold down the mouse button, and drag a rectangle of about half the size of the artboard. When the mouse button is released, the rectangle is created and automatically filled with the current fill color. The current fill and stroke colors appear in swatches at the bottom of the **Tools** panel, as shown in **Figure 4-9.** If the current fill color is white, the rectangle may not appear to be filled as the artboard is white, but it is filled. Also, notice the **Control** panel has changed to display options for the selected shape (the rectangle).

29. Click the color swatch for the fill color on the **Control** panel. A panel is displayed containing multiple color swatches, as shown in **Figure 4-10.**

30. Hover the cursor over each swatch to reveal the color name as help text.

31. Click the RGB Red color swatch to apply a solid red fill to the rectangle. Then, press the [Esc] key to close the color swatch panel.

32. Applying what you have learned, use the stroke color swatch on the **Control** panel to change the stroke to a dark green. The stroke is a line shape or the outline of a shape.

33. Click the **Stroke:** link on the **Control** panel. Notice the link is underlined. Underlined words are links to contextual panels. In this case, the stroke panel is displayed.

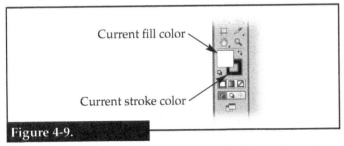

Current fill color

Current stroke color

Figure 4-9.

The current fill and stroke swatches indicate the colors that will be used for new shapes.

Copyright Goodheart-Willcox Co., Inc. For individual use only—reproduction or duplication of this copyrighted material is prohibited.

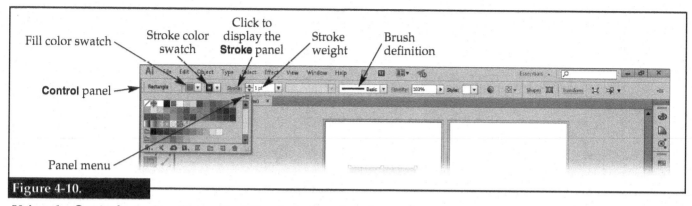

Fill color swatch • Stroke color swatch • Click to display the **Stroke** panel • Stroke weight • Brush definition

Control panel →

Panel menu →

Figure 4-10.

Using the **Control** panel to change the fill and stroke colors for a selected shape.

TIP
The [Ctrl][S] key combination can be used to quickly save a file. The file is saved in the background using the current name. If the file has not yet been saved for the first time, the **Save As** dialog box appears.

Layers

Create New Layer

TIP
Most panels have a "new" button, although the name varies from panel to panel. This button is used to create new swatches, colors, symbols, brushes, and other items on the corresponding panels.

Ellipse Tool

34. Click in the **Weight:** text box in the stroke panel, change the value to 50, and press the [Enter] key. Notice that the outline of the rectangle is now much thicker and the panel is closed. The *weight* is the thickness of the stroke.

35. Save your work by clicking **File>Save** on the **Application** bar.

Layers

Layers are like invisible sheets of paper stacked on top of each other, and each sheet can have different drawing shapes placed on it. The layers can be moved up or down within the layers stack to change the placement of shapes. Shapes placed on the top layers will appear in front of shapes on the bottom layers. The **Layers** panel is used to rearrange the order of layers in the stack. Layers exist in the drawing across all artboards. In other words, an artboard cannot have a unique set of layers that is not shared with other artboards. The **Layers** panel uses multiple icons to show the designer information, as shown in **Figure 4-11A**. Notice the template icon in the visibility section. The Circles layer is a template layer that is locked. Locked layers cannot be changed until unlocked. The selected object is on the layer indicated by the enlarged target icon, which in this case is the Polygons layer. Target icon indicates which object is selected and will be changed on the layer.

36. Click the **Layers** button in the **Panels** bar to open the **Layers** panel. Notice the rectangle was placed on a layer named Layer 1.

37. Double-click the name Layer 1 to begin changing the name. Once the name is editable, enter Rectangle for the name, as shown in **Figure 4-11B**. Press the [Enter] key to finish changing the name.

38. Click the **Create New Layer** button in the **Layers** panel to add a new layer. Notice the new layer is named Layer 2 and placed above the Rectangle layer. Since it is above the Rectangle layer in the stack, any shapes drawn on Layer 2 will appear in front of the rectangle.

39. Applying what you have learned, rename the new layer as Circle.

40. Click the **Ellipse Tool** button in the **Tools** panel. This button is located in the flyout displayed by holding down the **Rectangle Tool** button. Notice that once you click the **Ellipse Tool** button, it replaces the **Rectangle Tool** button as the visible button in the flyout.

41. Hold down the [Shift] key, click anywhere on the artboard containing the rectangle, and drag to draw a circle of any size. Holding the [Shift] key while drawing an ellipse constrains the shape to a circle. Also, notice the circle takes

For individual use only—reproduction or duplication of this copyrighted material is prohibited.   Copyright Goodheart-Willcox Co., Inc.

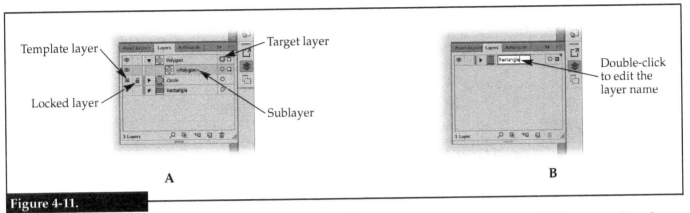

Figure 4-11.

A—The **Layers** panel provides information through the use of icons. B— Layers can be added, renamed, and reordered in the **Layers** panel.

TIP

Holding down the [Shift] key while drawing a rectangle constrains the shape to a square.

Selection Tool

Create New Sublayer

Selection Tool

Color

on the fill and stroke properties of the rectangle as that was the last shape edited.

42. Click the **Selection Tool**. Then click on the circle, and drag it so it overlaps the bottom edge of the rectangle.

43. Applying what you have learned, display the **Layers** panel.

44. Click and hold the Circle layer in the list, drag it below the Rectangle layer, and drop it. Notice the circle is now behind the rectangle on the artboard.

45. In the **Layers** panel, click the black triangle to the right of the Circle layer name. This expands the layer, as shown in **Figure 4-12**. Layers are composed of several shapes and colors. Each shape is saved as a sublayer to the main or parent layer. In this case, the sublayer is <Ellipse>.

46. Make sure the Circle layer is selected (highlighted) in the **Layers** panel, and then click the **Create New Sublayer** button on the **Layers** panel. Notice that a sublayer is automatically joined to a parent layer. It will always be beneath, or a child of, the parent layer.

47. Applying what you have learned, name the new sublayer Star.

Colors

48. Click the **Selection Tool** button, and click the rectangle to select it.

49. Click the **Color** button icon in the **Panels** bar to open the **Color** panel.

50. Click the None swatch located above the color spectrum, as shown in **Figure 4-13**. This removes the fill color from the rectangle.

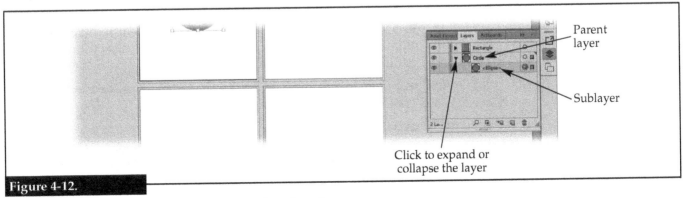

Figure 4-12.

A layer will contain sublayers for various drawing shapes.

Copyright Goodheart-Willcox Co., Inc. For individual use only—reproduction or duplication of this copyrighted material is prohibited.

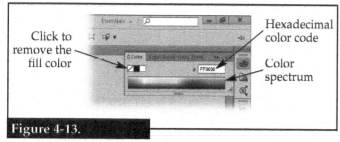

Figure 4-13.

Using the **Color** panel to remove or change the fill color of a shape.

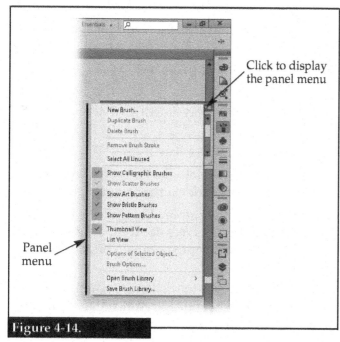

Figure 4-14.

Using a panel menu.

Brushes

51. Applying what you have learned, select the circle.

52. Click in a light-green area of the color spectrum in the **Color** panel. The fill color of the circle is changed to the green you picked. Notice the hexadecimal color code for the green that is shown in the upper-right corner of the **Color** panel.

53. Click in the text box for the hexadecimal color code, and change the code to 0000FF. Enter zeroes, not the letter O, but the letter F can be entered as uppercase or lowercase characters. When you press the [Enter] key, the fill color of the circle is updated to a color that has values of red 0, green 0, and blue 255. In other words, this color is pure blue.

Panel Menu

Most panels have a panel menu. This menu contains additional commands not displayed as buttons or settings in the panel. The panel menu button is located in the top-right corner of the panel.

54. Click the **Brushes** button to display the **Brushes** panel.

55. Click the panel menu button in the top-right corner of the panel to display the menu options, as shown in **Figure 4-14.** Notice the check marks next to the default brush categories. A check mark indicates the item is enabled. A disabled item is unchecked.

56. Click **Show Bristle Brushes** in the menu to disable this category. The brushes in this category will no longer appear as options in the panel.

57. Applying what you have learned, disable the pattern brushes category.

58. Applying what you have learned, enable the bristle brushes category.

Smart Guides

Smart guides are guidelines, locations, and comments that appear to help the designer properly align shapes. They are temporary guides and can be turned on or off. They are on by default.

59. Click the **View** pull-down menu, and make sure the **Smart Guides** menu item is checked. When checked, smart guides are enabled.

60. Activate the **Selection Tool**.

61. Hover the cursor over the center of the circle. A smart guide appears as an X at the center of the circle along with a comment specifying center, as shown in **Figure 4-15.** Also notice the coordinates of the center point are displayed in a separate box near the cursor.

TIP

The [Ctrl][U] key combination can be used to quickly turn on or off the smart guides.

For individual use only—reproduction or duplication of this copyrighted material is prohibited.

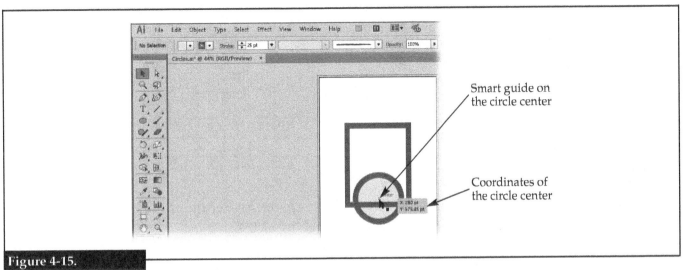

Figure 4-15.

Using smart guides to precisely locate shapes.

62. Hover the cursor over any of the four quadrants of the circle. A smart guide comment of anchor is displayed when the cursor is touching the anchor point along with the coordinates of that point. An X also appears on the anchor point.

63. Move the cursor along the edge of the circle. A smart guide appears as an X on the edge of the circle nearest the cursor. The comment is path. Notice that coordinates are not displayed for this smart guide.

64. Applying what you have learned, select the circle and move it across the rectangle. Smart guides appear when key points on the rectangle align with key points on the circle. Comments appear to indicate how the alignment will be applied.

65. Using the smart guides, align the circle so that the center of the circle intersects the bottom-right corner of the rectangle, as shown in **Figure 4-16.**

66. With the circle selected, click **Transform** in the **Control** panel to open the **Transform** panel.

67. Click in the height text box (**H:**), and enter 216, as shown in **Figure 4-17.** Since the units are set to points, this is equal to 3 inches (216 points ÷ 72 points per inch = 3 inches). Enter the same for the width (**W:**).

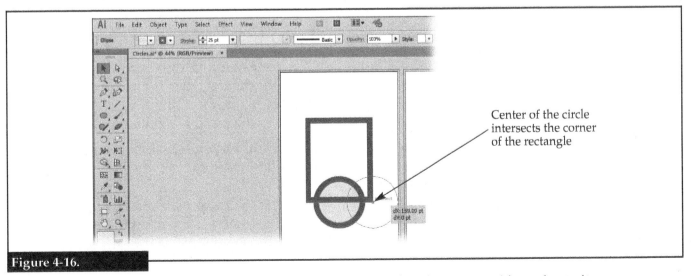

Figure 4-16.

Moving the circle shape to the bottom-right corner of the rectangle using smart guides to locate it.

Copyright Goodheart-Willcox Co., Inc.   For individual use only—reproduction or duplication of this copyrighted material is prohibited.

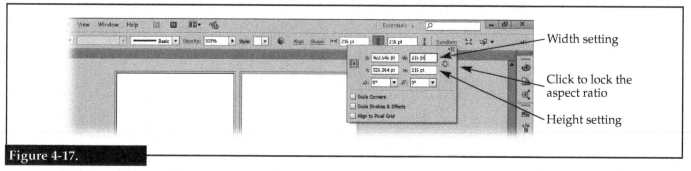

Width setting

Click to lock the aspect ratio

Height setting

Figure 4-17.

Setting a precise size for a shape.

68. Applying what you have learned, change the rectangle dimensions to 4 inches wide and 3 inches high. What are the values you entered?

_____

_____

69. Applying what you have learned, realign the center of the circle with the bottom-right corner of the rectangle to correct for any movement that occurred when resizing.

Color Guide

The **Color Guide** panel organizes color swatches according to harmony rules. Harmony rules are defined in the software to determine which will provide the best complement to a selected color.

70. Applying what you have learned, display the **Layers** panel and select the Rectangle layer.

71. Click the **Toggle Visibility** button (eye) next to the layer name to hide the layer. The layer is hidden, but it still exists in the drawing.

72. Select the Star sublayer in the **Layers** panel. This makes the layer the current layer. Any new shapes will be placed on the Star sublayer as long as it is the current layer.

Star Tool

TIP
Click **Edit>Undo** on the **Application** bar or use the [Ctrl][Z] key combination to undo the drawing and try again if needed.

73. Click the **Star Tool** in the **Tools** panel. The star tool draws a star from the center and expands outward. This takes a little practice to get good at drawing stars properly.

74. Click on the center of the circle, and drag. Keep the mouse button held down. Notice that the star has five points by default. Press the up arrow key until there are eight points. Then, drag to the edge of the circle and release the mouse button. Use smart guides to help precisely locate the star.

75. Applying what you have learned, use the **Control** panel to change the stroke of the star to 6 points in width and black.

76. Applying what you have learned, change the fill color of the star to #FF0000.

77. Display the **Layers** panel. Notice how each layer and sublayer has a thumbnail preview of what is on the layer. These thumbnails are automatically updated to reflect the current state of the layer.

78. Applying what you have learned, display the **Color** panel, and then click the **Color Guide** tab to bring that panel to the front, as shown in **Figure 4-18.**

For individual use only—reproduction or duplication of this copyrighted material is prohibited.   Copyright Goodheart-Willcox Co., Inc.

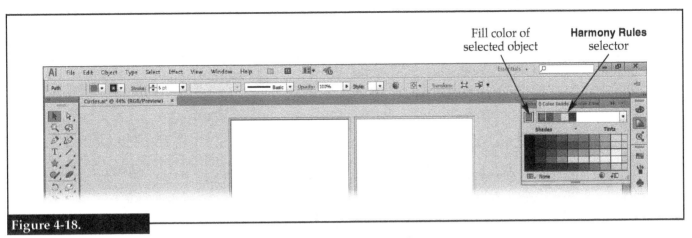

Fill color of selected object

Harmony Rules selector

Figure 4-18.

Using the **Color Guide** panel to select colors based on harmony rules.

79. Select the star shape, and examine the **Color Guide** panel. The fill color of the selected shape appears in the color swatch in the upper-left corner. Clicking this color swatch sets the fill color of the selected shape as the base color for the harmony rules.

80. Click the color swatch in the upper-left corner of the **Color Guide** panel. If you hover the cursor over this swatch, the help text is Set base color to the current color.

81. Click the **Harmony Rules** drop-down arrow. Scroll through the drop-down list to see the various rules that can be selected, and then click **Complementary** in the list. The swatches in the **Color Guide** panel are now only shades of red and shades of green.

82. Select the circle shape. You may need to first click on a blank spot on the artboard to deselect the star. Notice the upper-left color swatch in the **Color Guide** panel is now blue, but the harmony rules color swatches still reflect the complementary colors for red.

83. Click a light green color swatch in the **Color Guide** panel. The fill color of the circle is updated to that color, which complements the red of the star.

84. Select the star shape.

85. Look at the color swatches in the lower part of the **Color Guide** panel. Notice the labels above the swatches are **Shades** and **Tints**, and a downward-pointing triangle appears between these two labels. The triangle indicates the active colors included in the selected harmony rule. To the left of the triangle are color swatches that provide shades of the active color. To the right of the triangle are color swatches that provide tints of the active color. Shades are darker than the active color, while tints are lighter.

86. Click the red swatch that is 70% (two shades) darker than the original red in the star.

87. Applying what you have learned, change the fill of the circle to be tinted with the 90% (lightest) green tint.

88. Applying what you have learned, unhide the Rectangle layer. You can see that while the rectangle was not visible when the layer was hidden, it was still included in the drawing.

TIP

Shade and tint values do not appear as help text. Unless the default scale is changed in the **Color Guide** panel menu, the values from left to right are: 90% shade, 70% shade, 50% shade, 30% shade, hue color, 30% tint, 50% tint, 70% tint, and 90% tint.

Copyright Goodheart-Willcox Co., Inc.   For individual use only—reproduction or duplication of this copyrighted material is prohibited.

Swatch Libraries

The **Swatches** panel holds color swatches and pattern swatches. New patterns are stored as swatches in this panel as well. Patterns can be edited by double-clicking the pattern swatch in this panel.

89. Applying what you have learned, deselect all shapes.

90. Click the **Swatches** button in the **Panel** bar to open the **Swatches** panel.

Swatches

91. Click the **Swatch Libraries Menu** button in the bottom-left corner of the panel. A drop-down menu is displayed, as shown in **Figure 4-19.**

92. In the drop-down menu, click **Patterns>Nature>Nature_Animal Skins**. This library is opened in a floating panel.

93. Hover the cursor over each pattern swatch in the **Nature_Animal Skins** panel to see the name of each pattern. Click the Jaguar pattern swatch. This pattern swatch is added to the **Swatches** panel, and the pattern is also made the current fill color in the **Tools** panel.

94. Click the close button (**X**) on the floating panel to hide the panel.

95. Select the circle shape, and click the Jaguar pattern swatch in the **Swatches** panel. The fill color of the circle is replaced with the pattern.

96. Double-click the Jaguar pattern swatch in the **Swatches** panel. The view in Illustrator changes to pattern-editing mode and the **Pattern Options** panel is displayed, as shown in **Figure 4-20.** In this view, you can adjust the alignment of the pattern.

97. Click the **Tile Type:** drop-down arrow in the **Pattern Options** panel, and click **Brick by Row** in the drop-down list. This setting controls how the tiles of the pattern are aligned. Notice how the rows are now offset, and you can clearly see the breaks in the pattern.

98. Click the **Brick Offset:** drop-down arrow in the **Pattern Options** panel, and click **2/5** in the drop-down list. Notice the change to the pattern alignment.

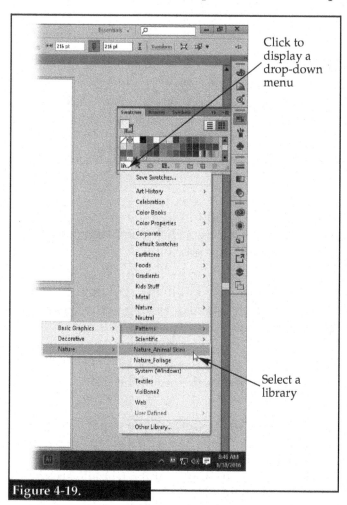

Click to display a drop-down menu

Select a library

Figure 4-19.

Selecting a library of color swatches.

99. Click the **Copies:** drop-down arrow in the **Pattern Options** panel, and click **3 × 3** in the drop-down list. The amount of pattern in the area is reduced. If there is a situation in which the pattern does not completely fill the shape, the **Copies:** value would need to be increased.

100. Hover the cursor over each button in the **Overlap:** area of the **Pattern Options** to see the name of each. There are two groups of buttons. The two buttons in each group are toggles. Only one button in each group can be active.

101. Toggle between the **Top in Front** and **Bottom in Front** options in the **Overlap:** area of the **Pattern Options** panel to see how the pattern changes.

For individual use only—reproduction or duplication of this copyrighted material is prohibited.   Copyright Goodheart-Willcox Co., Inc.

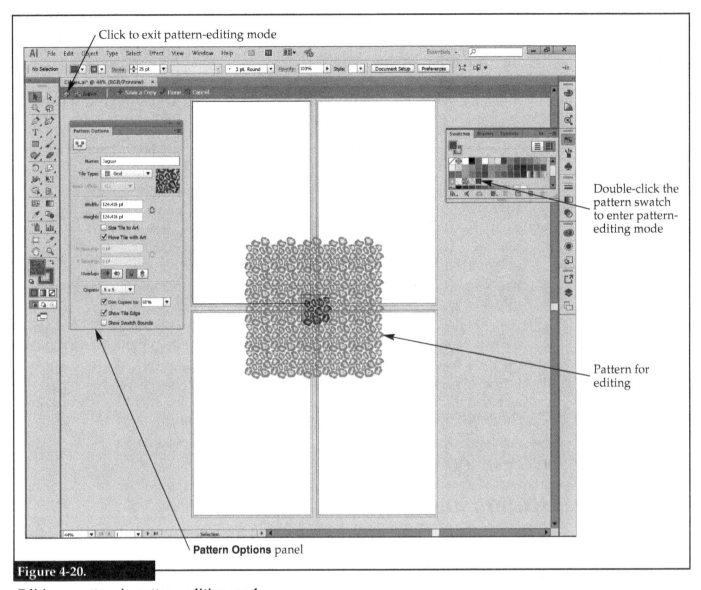

Figure 4-20.

Editing a pattern in pattern-editing mode.

**Exit Pattern
Editing Mode**

102. Click the **Exit Pattern Editing Mode** button (the arrow) or the **Done** link below the document tab to save the changes to the pattern and exit pattern-editing mode. The **Pattern Options** panel is automatically closed as well.

Canvas and Artboards

When this document was created, it was set up with four artboards each in portrait orientation. Each artboard can be modified at any point. How the artboards are placed on the canvas can also be changed.

Artboard Tool

103. Click the **Artboard Tool** button on the **Tools** panel. A label appears in the upper-left corner of each artboard indicating the name and number of the artboard. Notice that the name of the currently selected artboard appears in a text box on the **Control** panel. This text box can be used to rename the artboard.

104. Click anywhere on Artboard 4 to select it.

Copyright Goodheart-Willcox Co., Inc.   For individual use only—reproduction or duplication of this copyrighted material is prohibited.

**Delete
Artboard**

Landscape

Artboards

New Artboard

105. Click the **Delete Artboard** button on the **Control** panel to remove the artboard.

106. Select Artboard 3, click in the **Name:** text box on the **Control** panel, and change the name to Blank Page.

107. Applying what you have learned, use the **Control** panel to change the height of Artboard 2 to 8 inches and the width to 4 inches. What values did you enter?

_____

108. Select Artboard 2, and click the **Landscape** button on the **Control** panel. The orientation of the artboard is changed.

109. Click and hold Artboard 2, and drag it below the Blank Page artboard (artboard #3).

110. Applying what you have learned, move the Blank Page artboard below Artboard 1. Use smart guides to align the left edge with the left edge of Artboard 1.

111. Applying what you have learned, move Artboard 2 so its top edge aligns with the top edge of Artboard 1.

112. With Artboard 2 selected, click the **Artboards** button on the **Panels** bar to open the **Artboards** panel. Notice that Artboard 2 is selected (highlighted) in the panel.

113. Click the **New Artboard** button at the bottom of the panel. A new artboard is inserted on the canvas, as shown in **Figure 4-21.** Notice that the new artboard is identical to the selected artboard. Also notice that the artboards are renumbered based on their placement in the arrangement.

114. Applying what you have learned, name the new artboard Copy.

115. Press the [Esc] key to exit artboard-editing mode.

Rulers and Grid

Illustrator provides tools to help the designer in precisely locating shapes. Rulers can be used to help show the position of shapes on the artboard. The grid helps the designer align to the ruler and position graphics on the artboard.

116. Make the Blank Page artboard active. This can be done by clicking the artboard itself or selecting it in the **Artboards** panel.

TIP
The origin can be moved to a different location by dragging the upper-left corner of the ruler to a new location.

117. Click **View>Rulers>Show Rulers** on the **Application** bar. Rulers are placed along the top and right-hand side of the canvas. Notice that the origin (0,0) is the upper-left corner of the artboard. The default location of the ruler origin is the upper-left corner of the active artboard.

118. Move the cursor around the artboard. Notice there is a hash mark in each ruler that corresponds to the cursor location.

119. Make the Copy artboard active. Notice how the ruler shifts so the origin is at the upper-left corner of this artboard.

TIP
Changing the units of measure on the ruler does not change the overall units for the drawing.

120. Right-click anywhere on the top ruler. A shortcut menu is displayed that allows changing the units of measure for the ruler.

121. Click **Centimeters** in the shortcut menu. Notice that the units of measure change on both rulers.

122. Click **View>Show Grid** on the **Application** bar. Notice how the grid is applied to all artboards.

123. Click **View>Hide Grid** to turn off the grid.

For individual use only—reproduction or duplication of this copyrighted material is prohibited.   Copyright Goodheart-Willcox Co., Inc.

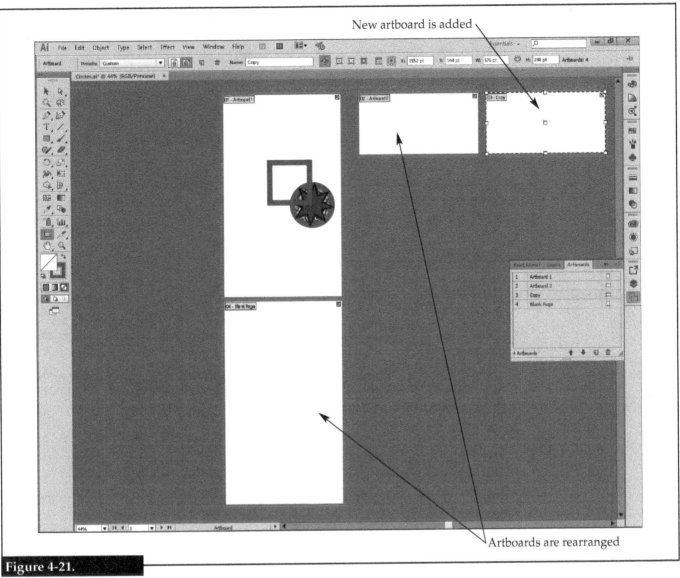

New artboard is added

Artboards are rearranged

Artboards moved around and new artboards can be added.

Line Segment Tool

TIP
The [Ctrl]['] key combination can be used to quickly toggle the grid display. The [Ctrl][R] key combination can be used to quickly toggle the ruler display.

124. Applying what you have learned, change the units of measure for the rulers to points.

125. Click the **Line Segment Tool** button on the **Tools** panel, and draw a horizontal line that starts on the left-hand edge of Artboard 1, extends through Artboard 2, and ends at the right-hand edge of the Copy artboard.

126. With the line selected, click **View>Guides>Make Guides** on the **Application** bar. The line is converted into a guideline. Any selected path, such as a circle, can be turned into a guideline using this method.

127. Click **View>Guides>Unlock Guides** on the **Application** bar. The guideline can now be moved. If this menu item appears as **Lock Guides**, the guidelines are already unlocked.

128. Select the guideline, and drag it up or down to the 144 point position on the left-hand ruler. As you drag, notice an indicator moves along the ruler to aid in alignment.

Copyright Goodheart-Willcox Co., Inc.   For individual use only—reproduction or duplication of this copyrighted material is prohibited.

129. Hold down the [Alt] key, and drag the guideline to the 72 point position on the left-hand ruler. Holding down the [Alt] key while dragging the guideline will make a copy, leaving the original in place.

130. Applying what you have learned, lock the guidelines.

131. Try to select one of the guidelines and move it. Guidelines cannot be selected or moved when locked.

132. Applying what you have learned, unlock the guidelines.

133. Select the guideline at the 72 point position, and press the [Delete] or [Backspace] key. The selected guideline is removed, but all others are retained.

134. Click **View>Guides>Clear Guides** on the **Application** bar. All guidelines are removed, even if the guidelines are locked.

Shape Builder

It is common to combine shapes to form a single shape. The shape builder tool is used to do this.

135. Applying what you have learned, draw a rectangle of any size on the Blank Page artboard.

136. Applying what you have learned, transform the rectangle so it is 1 inch wide and 3 inches high. Also change the stroke to 5 points and black. What values did you enter for width and height?

_____

137. Applying what you have learned, draw a circle that is exactly 1 inch in diameter.

138. Applying what you have learned, move the circle so that its center intersects the midpoint of the top side of the rectangle, as shown in **Figure 4-22**.

139. Click the **Selection Tool** button in the **Tools** panel.

Selection Tool

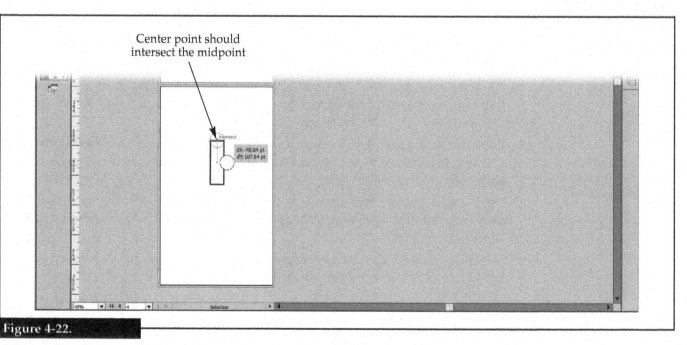

Center point should intersect the midpoint

Figure 4-22.

Moving the circle shape to the top midpoint of the rectangle using smart guides.

For individual use only—reproduction or duplication of this copyrighted material is prohibited.   Copyright Goodheart-Willcox Co., Inc.

**Shape Builder
Tool**

140. Hold down the [Shift] key, and click the rectangle and then the circle to select both shapes. They can be selected in any order. When both shapes are selected, they will both be surrounded by a blue box. If you click a selected shape, it will be deselected.

141. Click the **Shape Builder Tool** button in the **Tools** panel.

142. Move the cursor inside the rectangle. Notice how part of the interior of the rectangle is highlighted.

143. Click inside the rectangle, drag into the circle, and release the mouse button once all of the circle's interior is highlighted. The shape builder permanently joins the two shapes into a single shape as soon as the mouse button is released, as can be seen by the removal of the overlapping parts of the circle and rectangle. Only the outline of the new shape is retained.

144. Applying what you have learned, add a new artboard named Heart, and move it below Artboard 2.

145. On the Heart artboard, draw a 3.5-inch square. What value did you enter for the square dimensions?

_____

_____

146. Applying what you have learned, display the **Transform** panel. Click in the **Rotate** text box, and enter 45.

147. Applying what you have learned, draw two 3.5-inch-diameter circles centered on the top edges of the square.

148. Applying what you have learned, join the two circles and the square into a single shape, and then fill the new shape with red to create a heart, as shown in **Figure 4-23.**

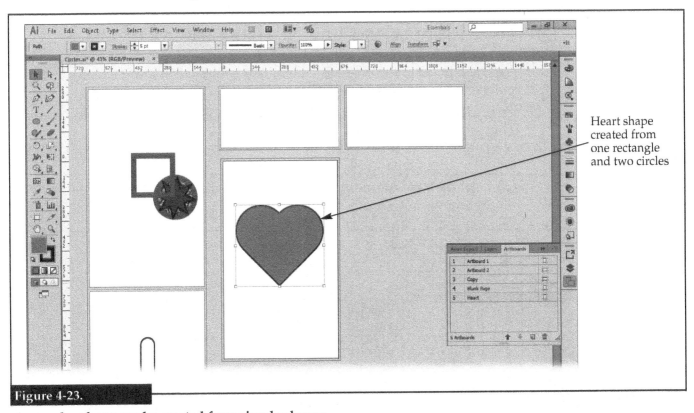

Heart shape created from one rectangle and two circles

Figure 4-23.

A complex shape can be created from simple shapes.

Copyright Goodheart-Willcox Co., Inc.   For individual use only—reproduction or duplication of this copyrighted material is prohibited.

Blend Tool

**Rounded
Rectangle Tool**

Illustrator has some very powerful tools. For example, the designer can allow an image or shape to blend from one shape to another. This is done automatically using the blend tool.

149. Click the **Rounded Rectangle Tool** button in the **Tools** panel, and click and drag to create a rounded rectangle that covers Artboard 2.

150. With the rectangle still selected, notice the four circular handles, one near each corner. These are *live corner widgets* used to adjust the radius of the corners. Move the cursor over one of the widgets, click, and drag to change the radius of the corners to about 30 points, as shown in **Figure 4-24.** The radius value is displayed as help text near the cursor as you drag.

151. Applying what you have learned, use the live corner widgets to change the corner radius of each corner to 0.

152. Applying what you have learned, transform the rectangle to 1/2 inch wide by 1/2 inch high, and then move it to the top-right corner of the artboard. What values did you enter?

TIP

When transforming the width and height of a shape, make sure the **Constrain Width and Height Proportions** button (link) is off unless you want to lock the two values together so changing one automatically changes the other.

Eyedropper Tool

153. With the rectangle selected, click the **Eyedropper Tool** button on the **Tools** panel, and click the heart shape. The eyedropper tool samples the color of a shape (the heart) and applies it to the selected shape (the rectangle).

154. Applying what you have learned, create a circle in the bottom right corner of Artboard 2 that is 1-1/2 inches in diameter. What value(s) did you enter and in what text box(es)?

Blend Tool

155. Change the fill color of the circle to blue.

156. Double-click on the **Blend Tool** button to display the settings for the tool.

157. In the **Blend Options** dialog box, click the **Spacing:** drop-down arrow, and click **Specified Steps** in the drop-down list. This setting allows you to enter a set number of steps between shapes.

158. Click in the text box to the right of the **Spacing:** drop-down arrow, and enter 4. This is the number of steps that will be created in the blend. When the tool is used with these settings, four new shapes will be created to blend both in color and shape from the rectangle to the circle.

159. Click the **OK** button to close the **Blend Options** dialog box and save the settings for the tool.

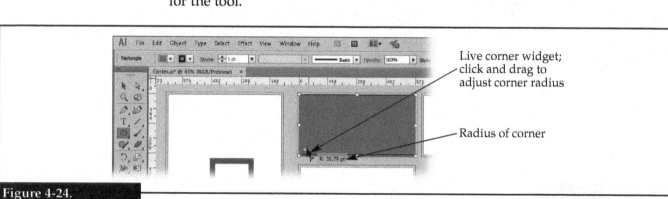

Live corner widget; click and drag to adjust corner radius

Radius of corner

Figure 4-24.

Adjusting the corner radius of a rounded rectangle shape.

For individual use only—reproduction or duplication of this copyrighted material is prohibited.

Copyright Goodheart-Willcox Co., Inc.

**Add Anchor
Point Tool**

**Direct
Selection Tool**

TIP
To select the
rectangle in the
blend shape, click
in the interior of
the rectangle (the
fill color).

160. With the blend tool active, click once on the rectangle and then click once on the circle. A series of four shapes is drawn between the rectangle and circle to create the blend. Notice how both the shape and color transform along the path, as shown in **Figure 4-25**.

161. Click the **Add Anchor Point Tool** button in the **Tools** panel.

162. Place the cursor between the rectangle and the circle. A path line is displayed when the cursor is over the path for the blend.

163. Click near the center of the path to add an anchor point at that location.

164. Click the **Direct Selection Tool** button in the **Tools** panel. The direct selection tool is used to select and modify paths within shapes, whereas the selection tool is used to select shapes.

165. Click the new anchor point, drag it to the lower-right corner of the artboard, and release. Notice how the steps in the blend are automatically moved to follow the path.

166. Click the **Direct Selection Tool** button in the **Tools** panel, and then click the rounded rectangle. Since the rectangle is now part of a blend shape, this tool must be used to select the rectangle instead of the selection tool.

167. Applying what you have learned, transform the width of the rectangle to 1-1/2 inches wide. Notice that the steps in the blend are automatically updated to reflect the change in the shape of the rectangle. What value did you enter for the width of the rectangle?

Custom Workspace

To this point, you have used the default Essentials workspace. However, most users find they like to customize the workspace to have the tools and panels in locations that suit them best and how they work.

Swatches

168. Click and drag the **Swatches** button away from the **Panels** bar so it is somewhere on the canvas. The panel is now floating as a collapsed panel, as shown in **Figure 4-26**.

169. Click the **Expand Panels** button (>>) on the collapsed **Swatches** panel to expand the panel.

170. Click **Edit>Preferences>User Interface...** on the **Application** bar. The **Preferences** dialog box is displayed with the **User Interface** category selected.

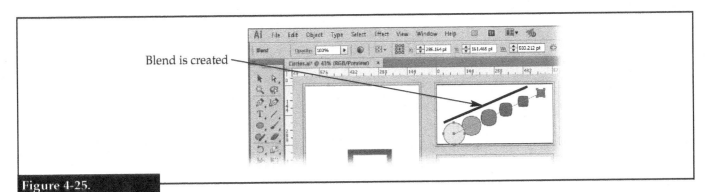
Blend is created

Figure 4-25.
A blend is a transition from one shape into another.

Copyright Goodheart-Willcox Co., Inc.   For individual use only—reproduction or duplication of this copyrighted material is prohibited.

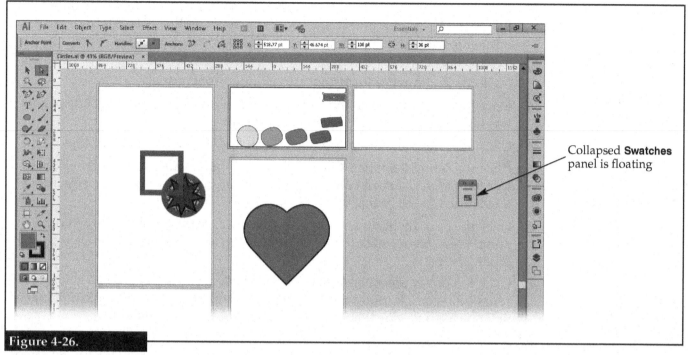

Collapsed **Swatches** panel is floating

Figure 4-26.

Panels can be dragged from the **Panels** bar to make them floating.

171. Click the **Brightness:** drop-down arrow, and click **Light** in the drop-down list. With this setting, your Illustrator screen should match the screen captures shown in this certification guide.

172. Click the **OK** button to set the changes and close the dialog box.

TIP
The settings in the **Preferences** dialog box are not saved in the workspace.

173. Click the workspace switcher on the **Application** bar, and click **New Workspace...** in the drop-down menu.

174. In the **New Workspace** dialog box, enter the name Floating Swatches Panel, and click the **OK** button to save the current configuration as a new workspace. Notice that the new workspace is automatically set as the current workspace.

175. In the workspace switcher, click **Essentials**. Notice the **Swatches** panel is no longer floating and has been returned to the **Panels** bar.

176. Use the workspace switcher to set the Floating Swatches Panel workspace current. The **Swatches** panel is now floating.

177. Save the file.

Export Artboards

178. Click **File>Export>Export As...** on the **Application** bar. A standard save-type dialog box is displayed.

179. Navigate to your working folder.

180. Enter Artboards in the **File name:** text box.

181. Click the **Save as type:** drop-down arrow, and click **Photoshop (*.PSD)** in the drop-down list.

182. Check the **Use Artboards** check box below the **Save as type:** drop-down arrow.

For individual use only—reproduction or duplication of this copyrighted material is prohibited.

183. Click the **Range:** radio button, and then enter 1-4 in the corresponding text box. This will export only the first four artboards.
184. Click the **Export** button.
185. Close Illustrator.

Lesson 4 Review

Vocabulary

In a word processing document or on a sheet of paper, list all of the *key terms* in this lesson. Place each term on a separate line. Then, write a definition for each term using your own words. You will continue to build this terminology dictionary throughout this certification guide.

Review Questions

Answer the following questions. These questions are aligned to questions in the certification exam. Answering these questions will help prepare you to take the exam.

1. Compare and contrast artboards and the canvas.

_____

_____

_____

_____

2. Describe workspaces.

_____

_____

_____

_____

3. What would happen to a shape if the stroke were changed from 1 point to 9 points?

_____

_____

_____

_____

4. After selecting a shape on the artboard, how is the weight of the stroke changed to 6 points?

_____

_____

_____

_____

Copyright Goodheart-Willcox Co., Inc.   For individual use only—reproduction or duplication of this copyrighted material is prohibited.

5. What is the importance of the order in which layer names appear in the **Layers** panel?

_____

_____

_____

_____

6. How is a layer hidden?

_____

_____

_____

_____

7. How is the **Color** panel used to remove the fill color from a selected shape?

_____

_____

_____

_____

8. List the five default categories of brushes that are found in the panel menu on the **Brushes** panel.

_____

_____

_____

_____

_____

9. Where on the **Application** bar is the setting for enabling or disabling smart guides?

_____

10. What are harmony rules for colors, and in which panel are they used?

_____

_____

_____

_____

11. Compare and contrast shades and tints.

_____

_____

_____

_____

For individual use only—reproduction or duplication of this copyrighted material is prohibited.   Copyright Goodheart-Willcox Co., Inc.

12. How is a pattern modified?

_____

_____

_____

_____

13. Briefly describe how to rearrange the artboards on the canvas.

_____

_____

_____

_____

14. When a new artboard is created using the **Artboards** panel, on what is the size of the new artboard based?

_____

_____

_____

_____

15. Where is the default location of the ruler origin?

_____

_____

_____

_____

16. Describe what the shape builder tool is used to do.

_____

_____

_____

_____

17. When using the blend tool, what does the steps setting control?

_____

_____

_____

_____

18. How are the settings for a specific tool accessed?

_____

_____

_____

_____

Copyright Goodheart-Willcox Co., Inc.   For individual use only—reproduction or duplication of this copyrighted material is prohibited.

19. After a workspace has been customized, how can the configuration be saved?

_____

_____

_____

_____

20. Preferences are not saved in a workspace, but how are they set?

_____

_____

_____

_____

For individual use only—reproduction or duplication of this copyrighted material is prohibited.

Copyright Goodheart-Willcox Co., Inc.

Lesson 5
Vector Images

Objectives

Students will create composite shapes from primitive shapes. Students will explain the Gestalt principle. Students will describe how to create and modify symbols. Students will modify primitives to create new shapes. Students will discuss how to edit Bézier curves. Students will describe the purpose of trim marks. Students will explain the function of the blob brush tool. Students will create a mirror image of a drawing. Students will clean up the unused colors in a file.

Situation

The Nocturnal Interactive Computer Entertainment (NICE) company has assigned you the task of creating the artwork for two cartoon characters that will appear in a new video game. The artwork you create will be used in printed materials and also for promotional T-shirts. In order to create the characters, you will need to know how to create primitives, composites, and symbols as well as be able to modify each.

How to Begin

1. Launch Adobe Illustrator.
2. Applying what you have learned, start a new project named *LastName*_Drawing using the Art & Illustration profile. Accept all default settings for this profile. This will create a document in RGB color mode with a single artboard that is 960 points by 560 points.
3. If the units of measurement are not set up as points, apply what you have learned and change the units to points.
4. Save the file as *LastName*_Drawing in your working folder.

Primitives

Primitives are basic shapes that can be arranged and stacked to form a complex shape. A *composite shape* is a shape composed of multiple primitives. In Adobe Illustrator, drawing primitives include rectangle, rounded rectangle, ellipse, polygon, and star. You have already created some of these primitives. Now you will use primitives to create a composite shape of a cartoon face.

Ellipse Tool

5. Click the **Ellipse Tool** button on the **Tools** panel.
6. Draw an oval of any size on the artboard. This primitive will be the face in the composite shape.
7. Applying what you have learned, move the ellipse so it is roughly centered on the artboard.

Copyright Goodheart-Willcox Co., Inc.   For individual use only—reproduction or duplication of this copyrighted material is prohibited.

Swatch Options

8. Click the fill color drop-down arrow on the **Control** panel, and click the **Swatch Options** button at the bottom of the panel. The **Swatch Options** dialog box is displayed, as shown in **Figure 5-1.** This dialog box is used to create a new, custom color swatch.

9. Click in the **Swatch Name:** text box, and enter Skin Color.

Preview of the new color

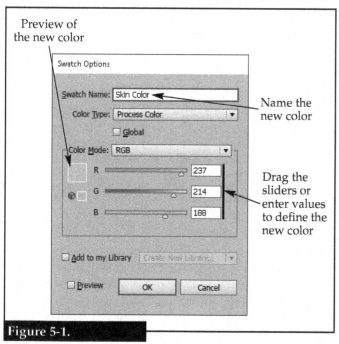

Name the new color

Drag the sliders or enter values to define the new color

Figure 5-1.

Creating a new color swatch.

10. Click the **Color Mode:** drop-down arrow, and notice the different color modes that can be used. Select **RGB** in the drop-down list, if it is not already checked.

11. Use the **R, G,** and **B** sliders to adjust the color to be similar to your own skin color. Remember, this is a cartoon character, so you can be creative if you like.

12. Click the **OK** button to create the new color swatch. The new swatch is added to the top of the color swatches, both in the **Control** panel and in the **Swatches** panel. The current fill color is also set to this color.

13. Click the new color swatch to fill the ellipse with the new color.

14. Applying what you have learned, set the stroke color to black, and change the weight of the stroke to 3 points.

15. Applying what you have learned, transform the ellipse so it is 350 points wide and 270 points high.

16. Display the **Transform** panel, click in the **X:** text box, and enter 480. Similarly, enter 280 in the **Y:** text box. These are the coordinates of the center of the ellipse. The center of the artboard is (480,280).

17. Click **View>Fit Artboard in Window** on the **Application** bar. This zooms the view so the entire artboard is displayed.

Gestalt Principle

The *Gestalt principle* states that a creation is greater than the sum of its parts as the mind tries to unify different elements into a singular whole element. The drawing you are creating is a basic cartoon face. The oval you just created is the face element. Ears will be added to make this a composite image. Additional facial features will be added to make the completed composite image of a face. Creating a composite image demonstrates how the meaning created with a composite image is greater than the individual primitive shapes. Placement and order add value to each primitive. Placing primitive shapes in correct locations will add meaning to the overall image. Additional ovals such as ears and eyes need to be placed correctly to add meaning to the image. The mind of the viewer will naturally try to unify all of the elements into a familiar element: a face.

18. Draw another oval of any size on the artboard. This primitive will be one ear.

19. Apply the skin color as the fill and black as the stroke.

For individual use only—reproduction or duplication of this copyrighted material is prohibited.   Copyright Goodheart-Willcox Co., Inc.

20. Applying what you have learned, transform the oval so it is 72 points wide and 120 points high. What are these dimensions in inches?

_____

21. Applying what you have learned, align the center of the ear primitive to the intersection of the left quadrant of the face primitive, as shown in **Figure 5-2**. Use smart guides to precisely locate the shape.

22. Applying what you have learned, rename Layer 1 as Composite Face.

23. Expand the Composite Face layer in the **Layers** panel to show the two sublayers.

24. Rename the sublayer containing the small oval as Ear and the sublayer containing the large oval as Face.

25. Drag the Ear sublayer below the Face sublayer. Notice how the ear shape is now behind the face shape.

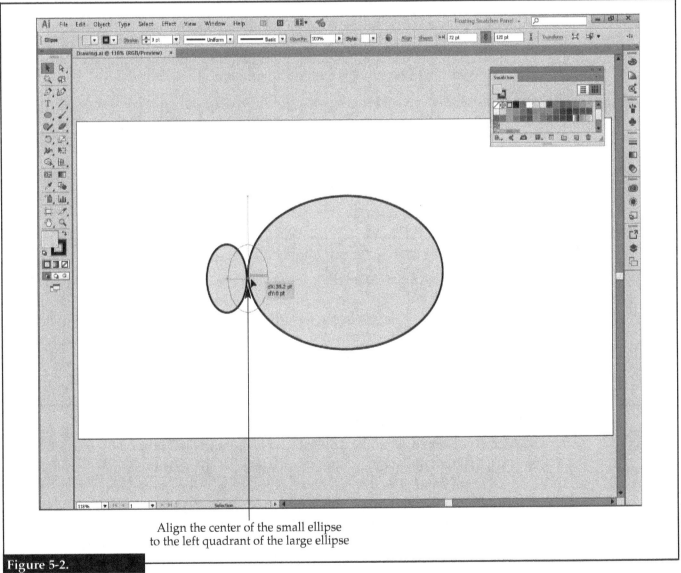

Align the center of the small ellipse
to the left quadrant of the large ellipse

Figure 5-2.

Using smart guides to align the ear (ellipse).

Copyright Goodheart-Willcox Co., Inc.   For individual use only—reproduction or duplication of this copyrighted material is prohibited.

TIP
The [Ctrl][C] key combination can be used to quickly copy a shape, and the [Ctrl][V] key combination can be used to quickly paste the contents of the system clipboard.

26. Select the ear shape on the artboard.

27. Click **Edit>Copy** on the **Application** bar. This places a copy of the shape on the system clipboard.

28. Click **Edit>Paste** on the **Application** bar. This creates a copy of the ear shape on a new sublayer named Ear. There are now two sublayers named Ear.

29. Align the center of the new ear primitive to the intersection of the right quadrant of the face primitive.

30. Adjust the sublayers so both ears are below the Face layer.

31. Applying what you have learned, change the name of the two Ear sublayers to be Ear_Left and Ear_Right. Be sure to match the name of the sublayer to the location of the primitive.

Symbols

Adobe Illustrator allows the artist to save a group of shapes as a custom symbol. A symbol can be used over and over again as needed. A symbol can be a movie clip or graphic. A movie clip is only used for importing into Adobe Flash. If it is to be used within Illustrator, the symbol is created as a graphic.

Symbols are often created on the canvas. The canvas can be used to draw elements of the scene and move them onto the artboard when finished. The advantage of drawing on the canvas is that the separate drawing will not interfere with the drawing on an artboard.

32. Use the scroll bars on the side of the screen to display an empty section of the canvas below the artboard.

33. Draw an oval on the canvas.

34. Applying what you have learned, create a new color swatch named White with a color of R255, G255, and B255. Apply this color as the fill color for the new oval.

35. Change the stroke color to black, and transform the size to 200 points wide and 100 points high.

36. In an area of the canvas next to the white oval, draw a circle that is 75 points in diameter. Fill it with your eye color.

37. In another area of the canvas, draw a black circle that is 40 points in diameter.

38. Click the **Selection Tool** button in the **Tools** panel.

Selection Tool

39. Click and drag a box around all three shapes on the canvas. A box appears around the objects to indicate they are selected.

**Horizontal
Align Center**

40. Click the **Align** link on the **Control** panel, as shown in **Figure 5-3**.

41. Click the **Horizontal Align Center** and **Vertical Align Center** buttons in the alignment panel. The three selected objects are moved so they are centered on each other both vertically and horizontally. You can now see how these shapes create a composite shape of an eye.

**Vertical
Align Center**

For individual use only—reproduction or duplication of this copyrighted material is prohibited.

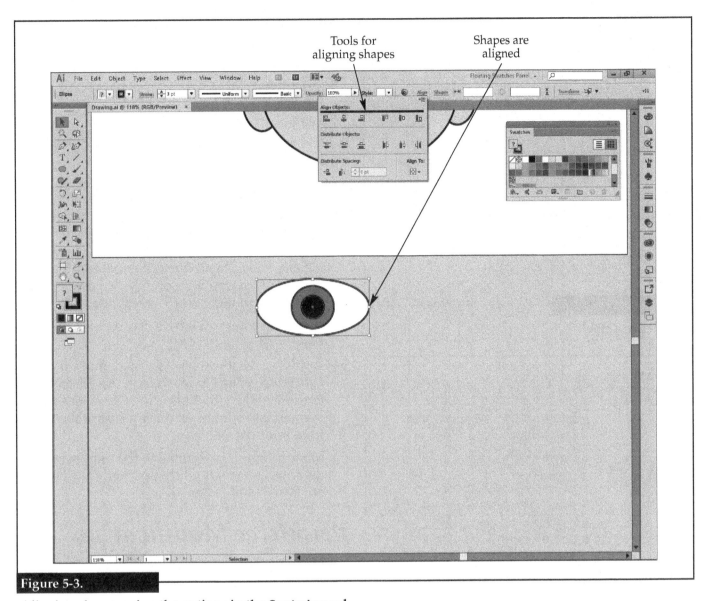

Figure 5-3.

Aligning shapes using the options in the **Control** panel.

Symbols

New Symbol

42. Make sure the eye composite shape is selected, and then click the **Symbols** button in the **Panels** bar to expand the **Symbols** panel.

43. Click the **New Symbol** button in the **Symbols** panel. The **Symbol Options** dialog box is displayed, as shown in **Figure 5-4.**

44. Click in the **Name:** text box, and enter Eye. This is the name that will be used to recall the symbol in the future.

45. Click the **Export Type:** drop-down arrow, and click **Graphic** in the drop-down list.

46. Click the **OK** button to create the symbol. The symbol appears as a swatch in the **Symbols** panel. The existing objects are converted to a symbol as well.

47. Display the **Layers** panel, and notice the sublayer for the symbol has been automatically named Eye, which is the name of the symbol.

48. With the symbol selected on the canvas, click in the **Instance Name:** text box on the **Control** panel, and enter Eye_Right. An *instance* is a copy of symbol, and each instance should have a unique name to help organize the drawing shapes.

Copyright Goodheart-Willcox Co., Inc.   For individual use only—reproduction or duplication of this copyrighted material is prohibited.

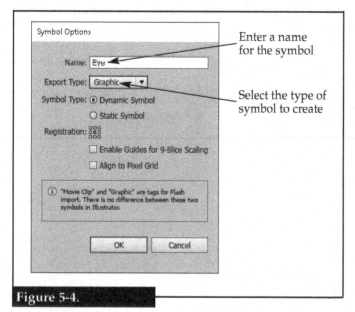

Enter a name
for the symbol

Select the type of
symbol to create

Figure 5-4.

Creating a symbol.

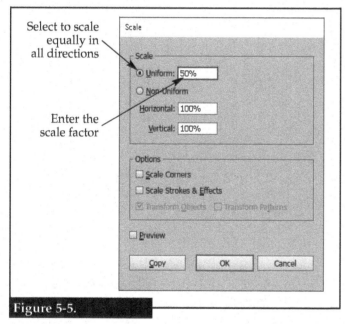

Select to scale
equally in
all directions

Enter the
scale factor

Figure 5-5.

Scaling selected shapes.

Star Tool

TIP

Shapes such as
rectangles and
ellipses can also
be drawn with the
single-click method
of displaying the
parameters dialog
box.

49. Display the **Symbols** panel, click the Eye symbol in the panel, and drag and drop it onto the canvas.

50. Applying what you have learned, rename the new instance of the symbol as Eye_Left.

51. With Eye_Left selected, click **Object>Transform>Scale...** in the **Application** bar. The **Scale** dialog box is displayed, as shown in **Figure 5-5.**

52. Click the **Uniform:** radio button, and enter 50% in the corresponding text box. Then, click the **OK** button to uniformly scale down the object by 1/2. Uniformly scaling means the object is equally scaled in all directions. Nonuniformly scaling means the object can be scaled differently in the X and Y directions.

53. Applying what you have learned, scale the Eye_Right symbol by 50%.

54. Applying what you have learned, move the Eye_Right symbol to an appropriate place on the left side of the face. This is the character's right eye and it should be on the left side of the face from your perspective.

55. Move the Eye_Left symbol to the right side of the face. Use smart guides to ensure the eyes are horizontally aligned.

Primitive Modification

Primitives provide a convenient starting point for creating composite shapes, but sometimes the shape of the primitive does not exactly match the needs of the design. Fortunately, primitives can be modified. To create the nose composite shape, which consists of a star and three ovals, the star primitive will be modified to meet the needs of the design.

56. Click the **Star Tool** button in the **Tools** panel, and single-click anywhere on the canvas. The **Star** dialog box is displayed, as shown in **Figure 5-6.** This dialog box is used to set the size and shape of the star primitive. When this dialog box is closed, the shape is drawn based on the parameters.

57. Click in the **Radius 1:** text box, and enter 25 pt.

58. Click in the **Radius 2:** text box, and enter 20 pt.

59. Click in the **Points:** text box, and enter 3.

60. Click the **OK** button to create the star primitive. Since the valleys are not very deep and there are only three points on the star, the resulting shape looks more like a six-sided polygon than a star. This primitive will be used as the bridge of the nose.

For individual use only—reproduction or duplication of this copyrighted material is prohibited.   Copyright Goodheart-Willcox Co., Inc.

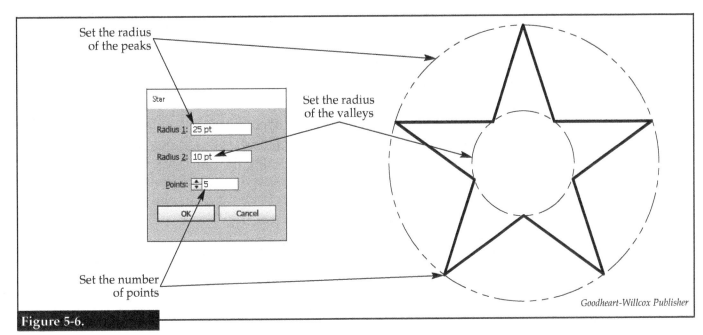

Set the radius of the peaks

Set the radius of the valleys

Set the number of points

Goodheart-Willcox Publisher

Figure 5-6.

Creating a star shape.

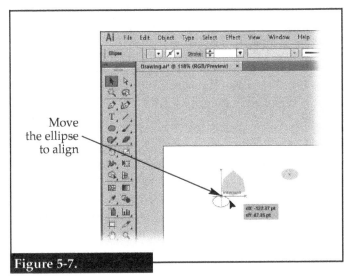

Move the ellipse to align

Figure 5-7.

Using smart guides to precisely locate the nostril (ellipse) on the nose (star).

61. Applying what you have learned, fill the star with Skin Color, and remove the stroke color.

62. Applying what you have learned, draw an ellipse that is 30 points wide and 20 points high. Fill it with Skin Color, and remove the stroke.

63. Move the ellipse so its center point aligns with the bottom and left points of the star, as shown in **Figure 5-7.**

64. Applying what you have learned, copy and paste the ellipse.

65. Align the center point of the pasted ellipse with the bottom and right points of the star. These ellipse primitives will be used as nostrils.

66. Create another ellipse that is 40 points wide and 20 points high. Fill it with Skin Color, and remove the stroke. This primitive will be used as the point of the nose.

67. Move the new ellipse so its center point intersects the bottom point of the star. You now should be able to see how the four primitives create a composite shape for the nose. To lock the primitives together, they can be grouped.

68. Applying what you have learned, select all four primitives that compose the nose by dragging a selection box around the shapes. Anything enclosed in the selection marquee or touching it will be selected.

69. Click **Object>Group** on the **Application** bar. The primitives are joined into a composite shape, but within the group the individual primitives retain their definitions.

70. Click **View>Outline** on the **Application** bar. The outline view displays the underlying structure of a vector drawing without showing the end result. The fills and strokes are not displayed.

TIP

The [Ctrl][G] key combination can be used to quickly group selected shapes. The [Ctrl][Shift][G] key combination ungroups the shapes.

Copyright Goodheart-Willcox Co., Inc.   For individual use only—reproduction or duplication of this copyrighted material is prohibited.

71. Click **View>Preview** on the **Application** bar. The preview view displays the end result of the vector drawing, which is the view you have been working in to this point.

72. Copy and paste the nose group, and drag it to the canvas.

73. Applying what you have learned, transform the nose copy with a uniform scaling of 125%. This makes the group slightly larger than the original.

74. In the **Swatches** panel, select the Skin Color swatch, and then click the **New Swatch** button in the panel. By first selecting the Skin Color swatch, its properties are automatically copied to the **New Swatch** dialog box. This is an easy way to create a new color swatch that is similar to an existing color swatch.

75. Enter Shadow in the **Swatch Name:** text box.

76. Click the **Color Mode:** drop-down arrow, and click **HSB** in the drop-down list. The hue, saturation, brightness (HSB) color model defines color based on these properties. Changing the brightness, or luminescence, setting creates either a shade (darker) or tint (lighter) of the color.

77. Adjust the brightness slider (**B**) to 80%.

78. Click the **OK** button to create the new swatch.

79. Set the fill color of the larger nose composite to the Shadow color.

80. Move the larger nose composite to the center of the face. Use smart guides to precisely locate the shape, as shown in **Figure 5-8.**

81. Click the zoom control drop-down arrow at the bottom of the Illustrator screen, and click 300% in the drop-down list. Then use the scroll bars on the right and bottom of the screen so the smaller nose composite is visible.

82. Select the smaller nose composite.

Isolate Selected Object

83. Click the **Isolate Selected Object** button on the **Control** panel. Illustrator enters isolation mode. *Isolation mode* allows for changes to be made to selected objects or layers without changing any of the surrounding items. Notice all shapes other than the smaller nose composite are ghosted, which indicates they cannot be selected. Also notice the toolbar that appears below the ruler. This toolbar displays the layer that is isolated and the group that is isolated. Additionally, the **Layers** panel contains an Isolation Mode layer and the selected group as a sublayer.

84. Select the smaller nose composite. Notice that the composite was automatically ungrouped when isolation mode was entered. This can be confirmed by clicking the **Object** pull-down menu and seeing that the **Ungroup** menu item is grayed out.

85. Applying what you have learned, select the left and right nostril primitives, change the stroke weight to 4 points, and set stroke color to the Shadow color. Notice the order of the shapes in the stack. The tip of the nose is in front of (or on top of) the nostrils, so it appears as if only half of each nostril has a stroke.

86. Click the **Brush Definition** drop-down arrow on the **Control** panel, and click **Charcoal Feather** in the drop-down list. The stroke is changed to this brush type. Also, notice the stroke weight is automatically changed. Leave it at the new setting.

87. Click the **Variable Width Profile** drop-down arrow on the **Application** bar, and click **Width Profile 4** in the drop-down list. This profile tapers the stroke from wide to narrow. The brush combined with the profile and the order of the shapes creates an effect of a dithered (broken) shadow on the nostrils.

For individual use only—reproduction or duplication of this copyrighted material is prohibited.   Copyright Goodheart-Willcox Co., Inc.

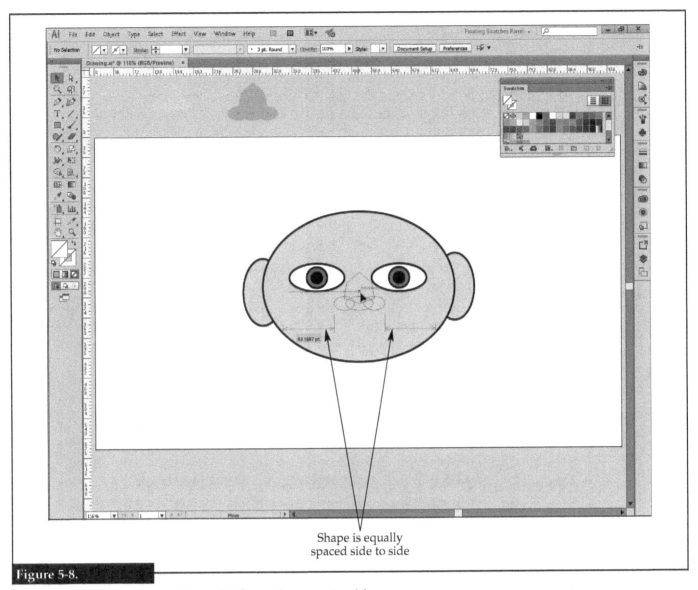

Shape is equally
spaced side to side

Figure 5-8.

Centering the nose composite on the face using smart guides.

Exit Isolation Mode

TIP

If you accidentally deselect the nose before changing the order, select the shadow and click **Object>Arrange> Send Backward** on the **Application** bar. Do this until the nose is in front of the shadow.

88. Click the **Exit Isolation Mode** button on the **Control** panel to exit isolation mode. The composite is automatically regrouped.

89. Click **View>Fit Artboard in Window** to see the entire artboard.

90. Move the nose group so it is centered on the nose shadow. Notice how the nose is behind the shadow.

91. Click **Object>Arrange>Bring to Front** on the **Application** bar. This will change the sublayer order so the selected shapes (the nose) are above or in front of all other shapes.

92. The arrow keys can be used to move a selected shape. If needed, select the nose and make any adjustments. There should be slightly more shadow below the nose than above it.

Copyright Goodheart-Willcox Co., Inc.   For individual use only—reproduction or duplication of this copyrighted material is prohibited.

Bézier Curves

A Bézier curve is a type of line composed of anchor nodes each with control points. The location of the control points and the distance each is from the anchor nodes influences the curvature of the shape. Think of the control points as magnets that pull the curve. The length of the line from the anchor to the control point is the strength of the attraction. Bézier curves are used to create smooth shapes. To create a smooth curve without a Bézier curve, the shape would need to be drawn with many anchor points and a straight line segment between each, as shown in **Figure 5-9.** In this case, a smooth curve can only be approximated by the straight line segments.

**Direct
Selection Tool**

93. Draw an ellipse on the canvas, fill it with Skin Color, and set the stroke to black with a weight of 3 points. In Illustrator, an ellipse is a type of Bézier curve.

94. Make the ellipse 100 points wide and 50 points high.

95. Click the **Direct Selection Tool** button in the **Tools** panel. This tool will allow you to modify the anchor points on the shape's path.

96. Click the anchor point at the bottom of the ellipse. Notice the selected anchor is filled blue, while unselected anchor points are filled white. Also, the control points are displayed for the selected anchor and the anchor on either side of it on the shape's path.

97. Click and drag any control point. See how the position of the control point influences the curve.

98. Click and drag a different control point. Notice how easy it is to create an interesting organic shape.

99. Click **Edit>Undo** in the **Application** bar to reverse the edits to the ellipse. Repeat this as needed until the ellipse is returned to its initial shape.

100. Click the bottom anchor point (not a control point), and drag it to the center of the oval. This shape will be used as an eyelid.

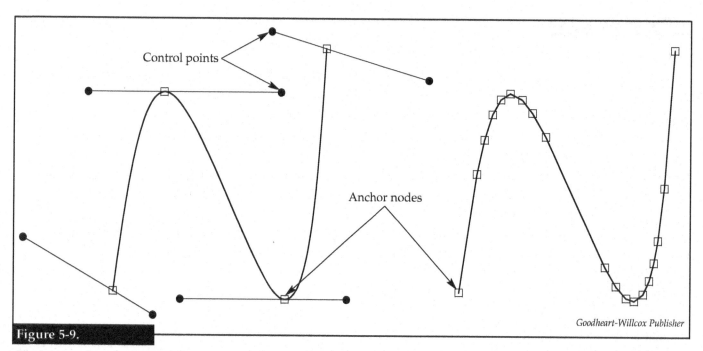

Control points

Anchor nodes

Goodheart-Willcox Publisher

Figure 5-9.

These two shapes appear identical, but the Bézier curve on the left is composed of far fewer anchor nodes or points. Also, the shape on the right only approximates a curve with straight line segments.

For individual use only—reproduction or duplication of this copyrighted material is prohibited.

Copyright Goodheart-Willcox Co., Inc.

Selection Tool

101. Click the **Selection Tool** button in the **Tools** panel, and then copy and paste a second eyelid. Clicking this button before copying ensures that the entire shape is selected, not just an anchor point.

102. Move each eyelid so the top of the shape intersects with the top of the eye, as shown in **Figure 5-10.** Notice how the character looks tired or sleepy, or perhaps even upset. The eyes and eyelids together play a large part of how emotions and moods are expressed.

103. Applying what you have learned, edit the bottom anchor point for each eyelid to reveal more of the eyes. Notice how the emotion of the image changes with the simple manipulation of a single part. This demonstrates the Gestalt principle as a single part movement changed the total feeling of the scene.

104. Applying what you have learned, draw an ellipse and edit it to create a simple smiling mouth. Fill the shape with red, and set the stroke to black. Move it into position on the face.

105. Applying what you have learned, create hair for the character from multiple primitives. Make the hairstyle for a man. Later, you will create a woman character based on this first character. Use a fill color that matches your own hair color. Create new color swatches as needed.

TIP

Remember, the **Undo** function can be used to quickly reverse edits. Try modifying the shape, and if you do not like how it looks, undo and try again.

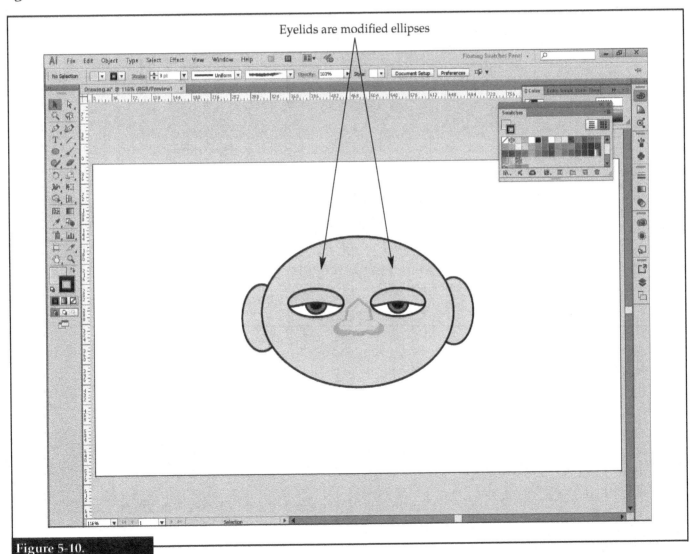

Figure 5-10.

Ellipses are modified and moved into place to form the eyelids.

Copyright Goodheart-Willcox Co., Inc.   For individual use only—reproduction or duplication of this copyrighted material is prohibited.

Trim Marks

TIP

Trim marks are shapes just like lines, rectangles, and ellipses. They can be moved, edited, and deleted. However, be aware of their purpose when modifying trim marks.

Artboard Tool

This character will be used on the packaging for a video game in which he appears. To help set up the image for printing, the publisher has requested all art be submitted with trim marks. *Trim marks* are lines appearing on the printed sheet showing where the paper will be cut or trimmed. The game also needs a female character. To save development time, the male character will be copied and modified with new features to create the female version.

106. Applying what you have learned, group all shapes in the face.

107. Click **Object>Create Trim Marks** on the **Application** bar. Thin lines are added at the four corners of the selected group, as shown in **Figure 5-11**.

108. Click the **Artboard Tool** button in the **Tools** panel, and select Artboard 1.

109. Use the zoom control at the bottom of the screen to zoom to about 50% so enough canvas can be seen to place a copy of the existing artboard.

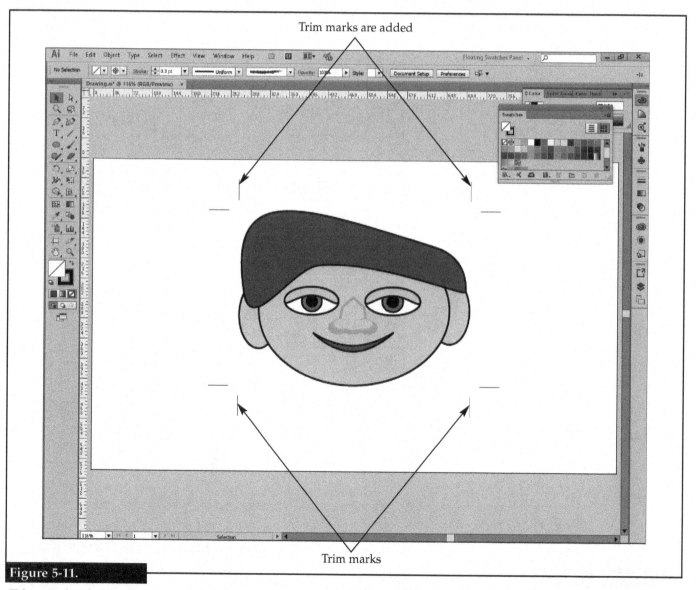

Trim marks are added

Trim marks

Figure 5-11.

Trim marks show where to cut the paper to the extent of the graphic.

For individual use only—reproduction or duplication of this copyrighted material is prohibited.

Copyright Goodheart-Willcox Co., Inc.

110. Hold down the [Alt] or [Option] key, click Artboard 1, drag it to the open canvas space, and release the mouse button and key. Holding down this key while dragging creates a copy of the item.

111. Applying what you have learned, rename the Artboard 1 as Male and the new artboard as Female.

112. Applying the skills you have learned, modify the mouth, eyelids, and hair on the Female artboard to create a female character. Use the zoom control as to better see the shapes, anchor points, and control points as you edit the character.

Line Segment Tool

113. Click the **Line Segment Tool** button in the **Tools** panel. This tool is used to draw straight line segments, as opposed to Bézier curves that are created with the **Pen Tool**.

114. Click and drag to draw a single eyelash. Repeat this as needed to add eyelashes to both eyes.

115. Hold down the [Ctrl] key, and click one instance of the Eye symbol for the female character. By holding down this key, you can select a shape within a group, in this case, the Eye symbol, without ungrouping the group.

116. Click the **Edit Symbol** button on the **Control** panel. Symbols can only be changed using this button. If a warning appears stating that you are going to permanently change the symbol definitions, click the **OK** button. The symbol is displayed in symbol-editing mode.

117. Select the ellipse that forms the color of the eye, and change the fill color to a different color of your choice.

Exit Symbol Editing Mode

118. Click the **Exit Symbol Editing Mode** button to save the changes to the symbol. Notice that the eye color has changed in *all* symbols. Each symbol is linked as an instance. A change to one instance is applied to all instances.

119. Select an instance of the Eye symbol on the male character.

120. Click the **Break Link** button on the **Control** panel.

121. Applying what you have learned, select the ellipse that forms the color of the eye in what was a symbol, and change the fill color to match your eye color. Repeat for the other eye on the male character.

Blob Brush Tool

The blob brush tool is used to draw freehand items with the mouse or drawing tablet. It is similar to the line segment tool, except the line segment tool draws a path only. The blob brush tool creates a filled-in shape and then adds a stroke around the fill. An advantage to using the blob brush tool is that compound or overlapping paths are automatically joined. The finished shape created with the blob brush can also be manipulated at each anchor point.

Blob Brush Tool

122. Double-click the **Blob Brush Tool** button on the **Tools** panel to open the **Blob Brush Tools Options** dialog box, as shown in **Figure 5-12.**

123. Click the **Fidelity** slider and drag it to the fourth notch (the far right). Also, enter 100% in the **Roundness:** text box. Then, click the **OK** button to save the settings.

124. Using the **Control** panel, change the stroke color to red and the weight to 5 points.

125. Using the mouse like a pen, click and hold and print your name below the appropriate character.

Copyright Goodheart-Willcox Co., Inc.   For individual use only—reproduction or duplication of this copyrighted material is prohibited.

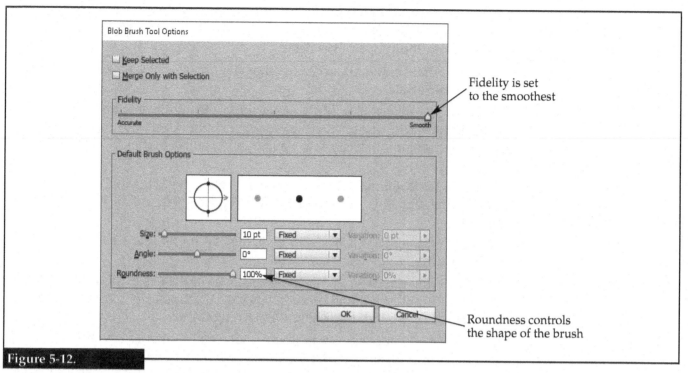

Figure 5-12.

Setting the options for the blob brush.

126. Print the name of your sister, brother, or a friend under the other character.

127. Click the **Selection Tool** button in the **Tools** panel, and select the first letter in one of the names. Change the zoom setting as needed to see the detail in the letter. Notice how the blob tool created the shape. One by one, select each letter in both names and examine how the tool created the shapes. Pay special attention to the point where lines of the letter intersect. Also, notice that the **Control** panel lists each of these shapes as a compound path.

128. Use the blob brush to create a mustache for the male character.

129. Use the direct selection tool as needed to modify the shape of the mustache.

Mirror Image

The client wants the characters to be printed on a T-shirt. The T-shirt printer uses a silkscreen process that requires the artwork to be in reverse. During the silkscreen printing process, the reversed image is transferred to the shirts so the images are right-reading. Illustrator has tools that make creating a reverse image, or a mirror image, an easy process.

130. Save the file. Then, click **File>Save As...**, and name the new file *LastName*_Shirt. This creates a copy of the file under a new name. The original drawing is maintained under the original file name. The open file is the copy, not the original.

131. Select one of the trim marks around the male character, and press the [Delete] key to remove the trim marks. Also remove the trim marks from around the female character.

132. Applying what you have learned, select the entire face and name for the male character.

133. Click **Object>Transform>Reflect...** on the **Application** bar.

For individual use only—reproduction or duplication of this copyrighted material is prohibited.

134. In the **Reflect** dialog box that is displayed, click the **Vertical** radio button in the **Axis** area. This sets the line about which the image will be mirrored. A vertical axis mirrors the image left to right, while a horizontal axis mirrors the image top to bottom.

135. Click the **OK** button to mirror the image, as shown in **Figure 5-13**.

136. Applying what you have learned, reflect the image and name for the female character about a vertical axis.

137. Click **File>Print...** on the **Application** bar. The **Print** dialog box is displayed.

138. In the **General** area of the dialog box, enter 1 in the **Copies:** text box and click the **All** radio button next to **Artboards:**. Then, click the **Print** button to print both artboards.

139. Hold the printed pages in front of a mirror or other reflective surface to see how the image and words are readable.

Shapes are mirrored

Figure 5-13.

Creating a reverse-reading (mirror) image.

Copyright Goodheart-Willcox Co., Inc.   For individual use only—reproduction or duplication of this copyrighted material is prohibited.

File Cleanup

Before exporting a file, the designer should clean it up. One reason for doing this is to make the file size as small as possible, but a cleaner file is also easier for others to use. One item that can be easily cleaned up is color swatches. By removing any unused color swatches from the **Swatches** panel, the swatches that were used are much easier to find and reuse. The printer will quickly be able to identify and mix the ink colors needed for the T-shirts.

140. Expand the **Swatches** panel, if it is not already.

141. Click the panel menu button located in the top-right corner of the panel.

142. Click **Select All Unused** in the drop-down menu. All color swatches that are not used in this drawing are selected in the panel, as shown in **Figure 5-14.** Selected swatches are outlined in white.

Delete Swatch

143. Click the **Delete Swatch** button at the bottom of the **Swatches** panel, and click the **Yes** button in the warning that appears. The selected color swatches are removed from the panel.

144. Applying what you have learned, open the **Save As** dialog box.

145. Click the **Save as type:** drop-down arrow, and click **SVG Compressed** in the drop-down list. This is a scalable vector graphic file type that is compressed and it will have a .svgz file extension.

146. Enter *LastName_*SVG in the **File name:** text box.

147. Navigate to your working folder, and save the file. Accept all of the default settings for the SVG file type.

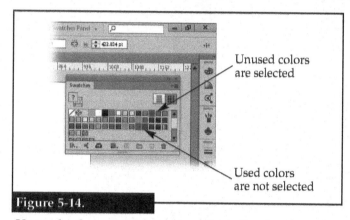

Figure 5-14.
Unused color swatches can be selected and removed from the **Swatches** panel.

148. Applying what you have learned, save the file as an Illustrator file (AI) in your working folder with the name of *LastName_*Backward Compatible. In the **Illustrator Options** dialog box that appears, click the **Version:** drop-down arrow, and click **Illustrator CS5** in the drop-down list. This will allow users of Illustrator CS5, CS6, and CC to open and use the file. Note: some formatting changes may occur as noted in the **Warnings** section at the bottom of the dialog box.

149. Click the **OK** button to close the **Illustrator Options** dialog box and complete the save.

150. Close Illustrator.

Lesson 5 Review

In a word processing document or on a sheet of paper, list all of the *key terms* in this lesson. Place each term on a separate line. Then, write a definition for each term using your own words. You will continue to build this terminology dictionary throughout this certification guide.

Review Questions

Answer the following questions. These questions are aligned to questions in the certification exam. Answering these questions will help prepare you to take the exam.

1. Compare and contrast composite shapes and primitive shapes.

2. How did the shape of the mouth demonstrate the Gestalt principle?

3. What would a digital artist do to a complex group of objects if the group is to be reused many times in the document?

4. Describe the basic process for modifying a symbol.

5. How can a symbol be converted to a group of shapes?

6. If a symbol is created as a movie clip, which other Adobe application can use the symbol?

Copyright Goodheart-Willcox Co., Inc.   For individual use only—reproduction or duplication of this copyrighted material is prohibited.

7. When using a drawing tool such as the **Star Tool** or **Rectangle Tool** button, what happens if you single-click to draw the shape?

_____

_____

_____

_____

8. How is the shape of a Bézier curve controlled?

_____

_____

_____

_____

9. What is the benefit of using a Bézier curve over drawing the curve with the line segment tool?

_____

_____

_____

_____

10. How can an ellipse shape in Illustrator be modified to change the shape?

_____

_____

_____

_____

11. What purpose do trim marks serve?

_____

_____

_____

_____

12. Describe how the blob brush tool creates a shape.

_____

_____

_____

_____

For individual use only—reproduction or duplication of this copyrighted material is prohibited.

13. After selecting a compound path created with the blob brush, how can the stroke color be changed without changing the fill color?

_____

_____

_____

_____

14. How can an Illustrator drawing be mirrored for use on a rubber stamp?

_____

_____

_____

_____

15. How are unused color swatches removed from the **Swatches** panel?

_____

_____

_____

_____

Copyright Goodheart-Willcox Co., Inc.   For individual use only—reproduction or duplication of this copyrighted material is prohibited.

Lesson 6
Gradients

Objectives

Students will explain gradients. Students will simulate a volumetric object using a two-dimensional shape. Students will describe cues that identify spatial objects. Students will compare and contrast radial and linear gradients. Students will simulate three-dimensional objects. Students will simulate rotation of an object about the X, Y, and Z axes. Students will combine effects on a single shape. Students will explain perspective drawing. Students will compare and contrast proofing options for print and screen. Students will export files for use on websites and mobile devices.

Situation

The Nocturnal Interactive Computer Entertainment (NICE) company is considering creating video games in which the graphics appear to be three dimensional, but the game engine uses two-dimensional graphics. You are tasked with learning how to represent three-dimensional objects using two-dimensional shapes. Additionally, you must be able to export the graphics in formats suitable for printed pieces and for use on websites.

How to Begin

1. Launch Adobe Illustrator.
2. Start a new project named *LastName*_Spheres using the default values for the Art & Illustration profile.

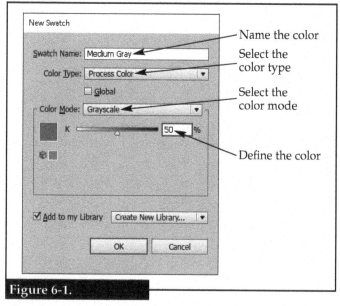

Figure 6-1.

Creating a new color swatch.

3. Save the file as *LastName*_Spheres in your working folder.
4. Applying what you have learned, draw a circle in the top-left corner of the artboard that is 150 points in diameter.
5. Click the fill color drop-down arrow on the **Control** panel. Notice the two swatches that look like folder icons. Hover the cursor over each to see the name. These are known as color groups, which are a way to organize color swatches. The swatches to the right of the folder icon are the colors within the color group.
6. Click any color swatch in the Grays color group, and then click the **New Swatch** button at the bottom of the panel. The **New Swatch** dialog box is displayed, as shown in **Figure 6-1**. The new swatch will be added to the Grays color group.

For individual use only—reproduction or duplication of this copyrighted material is prohibited.   Copyright Goodheart-Willcox Co., Inc.

TIP

In practice, *process color* always refers to the CMYK color model. The term *process color* loosely refers to the printing process, and four-color printing uses the CMYK color model.

7. Enter Medium Gray in the **Swatch Name:** text box.

8. Click the **Color Type:** drop-down arrow, and click **Process Color** in the drop-down list. A *process color* is one of the basic colors in a color model that are mixed to create other colors. For printed pieces, the process colors are cyan, magenta, yellow, and a key color that is almost always black (CMYK). *Spot colors* are pure hues that are themselves a base color without mixing. Printers use spot colors when only one or two colors are being applied to the paper. This prevents errors trying to *register,* or line up, the four process colors.

9. Click the **Color Mode:** drop-down arrow, and click **Grayscale** in the list. This color mode limits the color to shades of black, which ensures there is no trace of the other process colors within this color.

10. Change the black (**K**) setting to 50%.

11. Click the **OK** button to create the new color swatch. The color should also be applied as the fill color of the circle. If not, click the new Medium Gray color swatch in the fill color panel.

12. Applying what you have learned, change the stroke color to None.

13. Applying what you have learned, copy and paste the circle.

14. Move the copy to the right of the original circle so that it is near the top-center of the artboard and vertically aligned with the original. Use smart guides to help locate the shape.

15. Create two additional copies. Place one copy in the top-right corner of the artboard vertically aligned with the first two circles. Place the other copy below and horizontally aligned to the center circle, as shown in **Figure 6-2.**

16. Click the **Type Tool** button in the **Tools** panel.

17. Click below the top-left circle. A flashing vertical bar indicates type can be entered. Enter the word Flat.

18. Click the **Selection Tool** button. The text should be automatically selected. If not, click the text to select it.

19. Drag the word so it looks centered below the circle. In this case, do not use smart guides.

20. Applying what you have learned, add labels for the remaining circles as Gradient and Volumetric in the top row and Spatial in the bottom row.

Type Tool

Selection Tool

Gradient

A *gradient* is a transition between adjacent colors instead of a sharp divide. A gradient will be applied to the second circle to give the basic appearance of volume. *Gradient stops* set the color and location for the colors being blended. By changing the location of a gradient stop, the designer can change where the solid color stops and the transition begins. The color transition occurs in an area called the *gradient ramp.*

Gradient Tool

TIP

Swatches can be created and saved for gradients. This is a convenient method for applying gradients that may be repeatedly used.

21. Click the **Gradient Tool** button on the **Tools** panel.

22. Click the circle labeled Gradient to apply a default gradient. Notice how the circle fades from white to black. This is a linear gradient. Also notice the gradient ramp that is placed on the shape and the two gradient stops on the ramp, one on each end.

Copyright Goodheart-Willcox Co., Inc.

For individual use only—reproduction or duplication of this copyrighted material is prohibited.

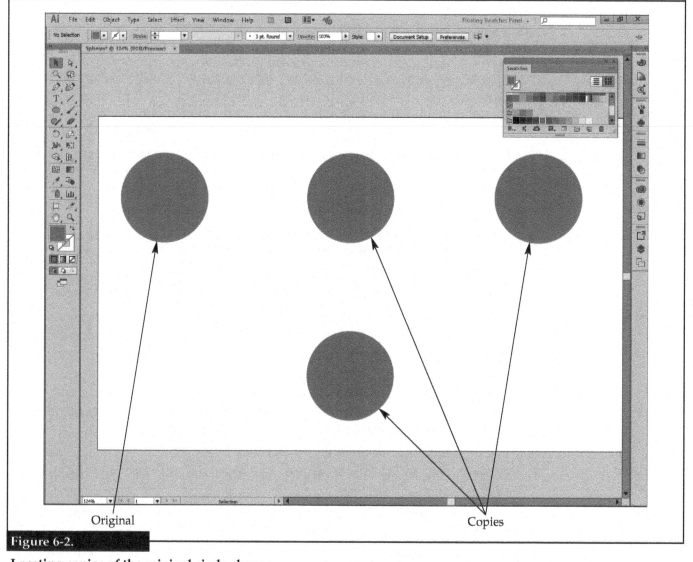

Original   Copies

Figure 6-2.

Locating copies of the original circle shape.

Gradient

23. Click the **Gradient** button in the **Panels** bar to expand the **Gradient** panel.

24. Click the **Angle** drop-down arrow, and click **–90°** in the drop-down menu. The gradient is rotated so it is vertical with the white spot at the top, as shown in **Figure 6-3**.

25. Click the gradient stop for the color black, either in the **Gradient** panel or on the shape. In the panel, the selected gradient stop has a black arrow top. The rectangle portion of the stop shows the color at that stop.

TIP
The location of a gradient stop can be precisely set by entering a value in the **Location:** text box.

26. Drag the gradient stop for the color black to the 80% location. The location is shown in the **Location:** text box in the **Gradient** panel. Notice a wider band of black is showing at the bottom of the shape.

27. Click the gradient slider located just above the gradient ramp, and drag it closer to the gradient stop for the color white. This slider shifts the center of the transition between the colors, so the transition becomes darker as more black is added.

For individual use only—reproduction or duplication of this copyrighted material is prohibited.   Copyright Goodheart-Willcox Co., Inc.

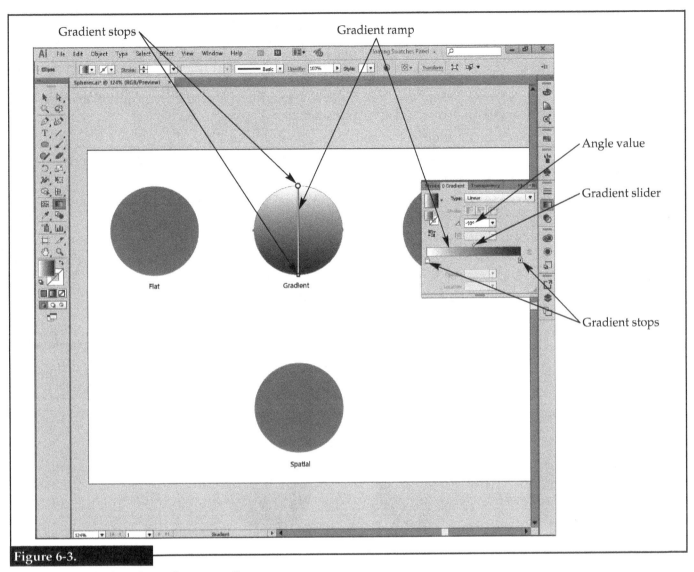

Figure 6-3.

Applying and adjusting a linear gradient.

Volumetric Simulation

A volumetric object is a three-dimensional object. It has volume. A volumetric object can be simulated in 2D with chiaroscuro. *Chiaroscuro* is an artistic technique in which the value of shadow and light are changed without regard for color along a shape to create the illusion of three dimensions. The value will range from a bright highlight to shadow.

28. Applying what you have learned, add a gradient at an angle of –120 degrees to the circle labeled Volumetric.

29. Set the location of the gradient stop for the color black to 85%. This will be the ambient color of the volumetric sphere. *Ambient color* appears in the dark areas of an object where the light source cannot provide direct illumination.

30. Set the location of the gradient stop for the color white to 5%. This will be the specular color of the volumetric sphere. *Specular color* or value is the highlight, or shiny spots on the object created by the light source.

Copyright Goodheart-Willcox Co., Inc.   For individual use only—reproduction or duplication of this copyrighted material is prohibited.

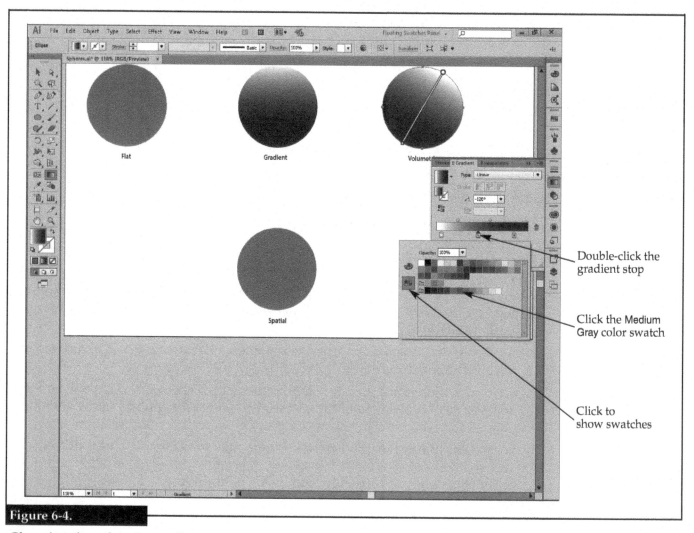

31. Move the cursor below the gradient ramp and between the gradient stops in the **Gradient** panel. Notice the cursor shows a plus sign (+). When this cursor is displayed, clicking will add a gradient stop to the gradient ramp.

32. Add a new gradient stop anywhere between the two existing gradient stops. Notice a second gradient slider is also added. A gradient slider will always appear between any two gradient stops.

33. Set the location of the middle gradient stop to 45%.

34. Double-click the middle gradient stop. This allows you to change the color of the gradient stop, as shown in **Figure 6-4.**

35. Click the **Swatches** button in the panel that is displayed. This gives you access to the new color swatch created earlier.

36. Click the Medium Gray color swatch. This will be the diffuse color of the volumetric sphere. The *diffuse color* is the main color for the object without any highlight or shadow.

37. Select the white-to-gray gradient slider, and set its location to 50%.

38. Select the gray-to-black gradient slider, and set its location to 50%.

39. Deselect the circle. Notice how the Volumetric circle looks much more rounded than the Gradient circle, but both are two-dimensional objects.

Swatches

Figure 6-4.

Changing the color of a gradient stop.

For individual use only—reproduction or duplication of this copyrighted material is prohibited.

Copyright Goodheart-Willcox Co., Inc.

40. Applying what you have learned, rename the existing layer as Circles.

41. Applying what you have learned, create a new layer named Background, and move it below the Circles layer. It is hard to see the specular highlights on the objects because the highlights and the artboard are both white. This layer will be used to provide greater contrast between the highlights and the background.

42. On the Background layer, create a rectangle that covers the entire artboard.

43. Change the fill color of the rectangle to RGB Blue. Notice how this color has high contrast with the shades of gray used on the circles.

Spatial Object

Spatial objects have volume, but also include lighting and other features that help the viewer determine where these objects are located in the space. *Backlighting* is used to help separate the object from the background. *Reflective lighting* produces a dimmer secondary highlight on the object from light reflected off another object or surface. A ground shadow is a feature that can be added to help provide contextual clues to the volume and spatial position of an object.

TIP
The Circles layer must be current in order to add a gradient to the circle.

TIP
Backlighting often can be simulated with a thin stroke of white.

44. Applying what you have learned, add a gradient at an angle of –120 degrees to the circle labeled Spatial.

45. Applying what you have learned, edit the gradient as shown in **Figure 6-5.** The left-hand gradient stop is #1.

46. Set all the gradient sliders to a location 50% between the stops.

47. Applying what you have learned, copy and paste the circle. Change the fill color to white, and move the circle so it is centered over the existing spatial circle, uniformly scale it to 102%, and send the copy to the back of the object stack. The copy simulates backlighting. Notice how the thin halo of white separates the object from the background. This is what backlighting does.

48. Applying what you have learned, group the spatial circle and the backlighting circle.

49. Applying what you have learned, add a new sublayer to the Circles layer, and name it Shadow. Move the new sublayer to the bottom of the sublayer stack.

50. Hide all layers and sublayers except for the Shadow, spatial sphere sublayer, and the Background layer.

51. With the Shadow sublayer active, create an ellipse of any size to the left of the spatial sphere.

52. Set the fill color to black and the stroke to None.

Gradient Stop	1	2	3	4
Location	10%	35%	75%	100%
Color	White	Medium Gray	Black	Dark brown, such as R117, G76, B36 or R96, G56, B19
Lighting Type Created	Specular	Diffuse	Shadow	Ambient

Goodheart-Willcox Publisher

Figure 6-5. Use this information to edit the gradient.

TIP

Clicking the
Opacity drop-down
arrow displays
a slider that can
be dragged to
dynamically
change the opacity
value.

53. Click in the text box next to the **Opacity** link on the **Control** panel, and enter 60%. Notice how some of the background color bleeds through the black fill of the ellipse. Opacity is a measure of transparency, or how see-through the color is. Opacity of 60% means the fill color for the ellipse is 40% transparent. This allows the fill color to blend with the background color. If you look at real shadows, they usually contain some of the color of the surface on which they appear.

54. Applying what you have learned, transform the ellipse to a height of 45 points and a width of 200 points. Since the light source is at an angle to the sphere (circle), the shadow will be a distorted shape of the sphere.

55. Move the shadow (ellipse) until the right-center anchor of the shadow aligns with the bottom-center anchor of the sphere (circle), as shown in **Figure 6-6.** Use smart guides to precisely locate these points. The shadow is called a *ground shadow* because it provides an indication of where the sphere is in relation to a surface (the "ground"). Since the shadow is attached to the sphere, the sphere appears to be resting on a surface.

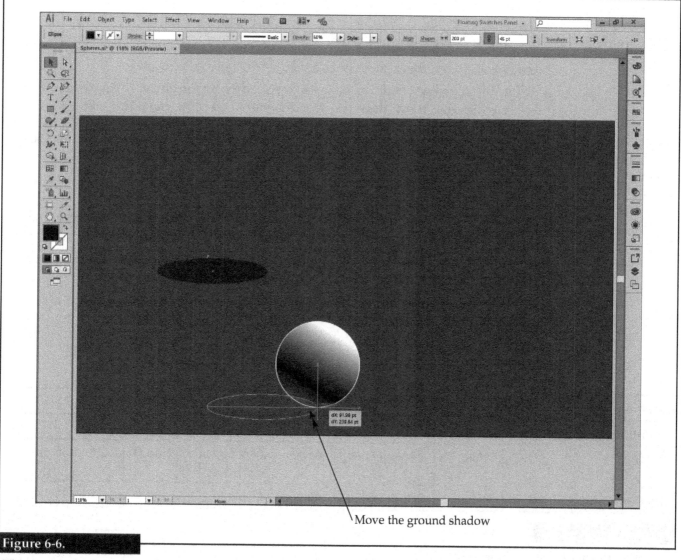

Move the ground shadow

Figure 6-6.

The position of the ground shadow provides a visual cue to the location of the sphere (circle) in space.

For individual use only—reproduction or duplication of this copyrighted material is prohibited.   Copyright Goodheart-Willcox Co., Inc.

56. Move the shadow down and to the left. Notice how the shadow gives different spatial information about where the sphere is located. The sphere now appears to be bouncing off the surface at an angle.

57. Applying what you have learned, transform the shadow to –30 degrees of rotation. Notice how this changes the spatial information not only for the sphere, but also the scene. Now the sphere appears to be bouncing off an angled surface instead of a horizontal surface.

58. Reveal all the layers. Notice how the use of value of shadow and light has changed the flat circles into much more interesting objects with the illusion of depth.

59. Save the file, and then save it as *LastName*_Radial in your working folder.

Radial Gradient

The gradients used to this point were linear gradients. A *linear gradient* creates a transition in a straight line. To further enhance the shadow, a radial gradient can be applied. A *radial gradient* creates a transition in a circular pattern, similar to the ripples produced by dropping a pebble into a pond. The goal of using a radial gradient for the shadow is to make the shadow more subtle.

60. Select the shadow, and display the **Gradient** panel.

Gradient

61. Click the **Type:** drop-down arrow, and click **Radial** in the drop-down list.

62. If there are any gradient stops between the left-hand and right-hand stops, select each one, and click the **Delete Stop** button on the panel. This button removes the selected stop.

Delete Stop

63. Applying what you have learned, change the color of the gradient stop on the left to black and the location to 0%. Notice that this is the center of the gradient.

64. Change the color of the gradient stop on the right to Medium Gray and the location to 100%.

65. With the right-hand stop selected, click in the **Opacity:** text box, and enter 10%. Notice how the shadow now blends better into the background with a softer edge, as shown in **Figure 6-7.** The effect can be refined by using the gradient slider to shift the position of the transition.

66. Applying what you have learned, set the rotation of the shadow to 30 degrees. This reverses the earlier rotation of the shape.

67. Move the shadow so the shadow center intersects the bottom of the sphere. Notice how the direction of the shadow no longer matches the position of the light source and highlight.

68. With the shadow selected, click **Object>Transform>Shear...** on the **Application** bar. The **Shear** dialog box is displayed. Shearing stretches a shape in the direction of a specific angle.

69. Check the **Preview** check box. This allows you to see the changes on the shape as they are made.

70. Click the **Vertical** radio button in the **Axis** area. This automatically sets the **Angle:** value to 90°. Since the light is coming down from above, this is the best direction to transform the shape.

71. Click the preview next to the **Shear Angle:** text box, and drag it until 333° is displayed in the text box, and release the mouse button. Notice how this stretches the shadow along the direction of the light.

Copyright Goodheart-Willcox Co., Inc.   For individual use only—reproduction or duplication of this copyrighted material is prohibited.

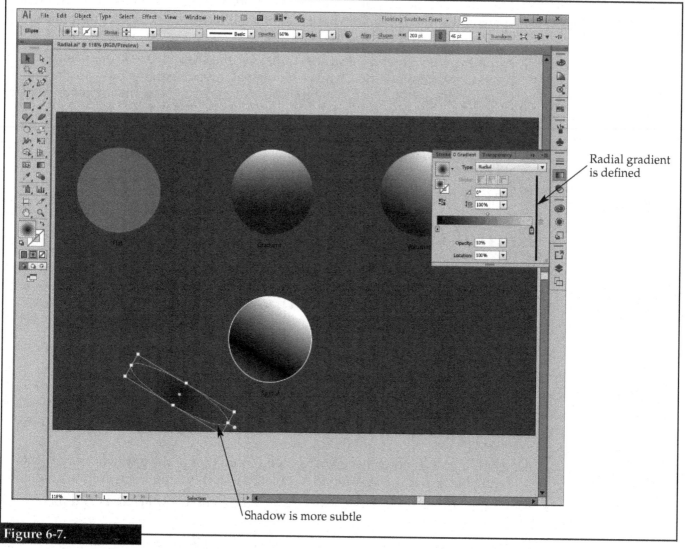

Radial gradient is defined

Shadow is more subtle

Figure 6-7.

A radial gradient creates a softer ground shadow.

72. Click the **OK** button to close and apply the effect.

73. Applying what you have learned, transform the shadow so it is uniformly scaled by 200%.

3D Simulation

As you have seen, Adobe Illustrator can be used to represent shapes as three-dimensional objects. However, instead of manually applying gradients and shapes to create the lighting and shadow, Illustrator has tools to automatically display shapes as 3D representations.

74. Select the circle labeled Flat.

75. Click **Effect** on the **Application** bar to display the pull-down menu, as shown in **Figure 6-8**. Notice the effects are divided into two categories: Illustrator effects and Photoshop effects. Both types of effects can be applied to objects in Illustrator. Photoshop effects are borrowed from Adobe Photoshop and perform the same functions as in that program.

76. In the **Illustrator Effects** section, click **3D>Extrude & Bevel…** to open the **3D Extrude & Bevel Options** dialog box, as shown in **Figure 6-9**.

For individual use only—reproduction or duplication of this copyrighted material is prohibited.

Copyright Goodheart-Willcox Co., Inc.

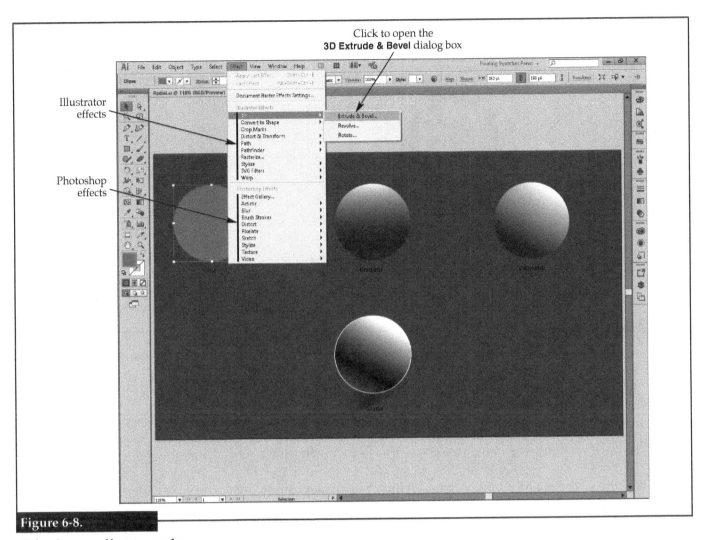

Figure 6-8.

Selecting an effect to apply.

TIP

If the preview causes the computer to run slowly, you may need to turn off the preview. You can always apply the effect to see how it looks, and, if needed, undo it and try again.

77. Drag the dialog box to a location that allows you to see the circle and the dialog box at the same time.

78. Check the **Preview** check box.

79. Click the **Position:** drop-down arrow, and click **Off-Axis Front** in the drop-down list. This is a preset option that will simulate the circle as a cylinder.

80. Click the **Extrude Depth:** drop-down arrow, and drag the slider that is displayed to see how the cylinder depth is changed. The preview on the shape is updated when the mouse button is released.

81. Click in the **Extrude Depth:** text box, and enter 144 pt, but do *not* press the [Enter] key. Pressing the [Enter] key will close the window. What cylinder height in inches is simulated by the value of 144 points?

82. In the **Cap:** area, click the **Turn cap off for hollow appearance** button. Notice the preview on the object shows the cylinder as hollow, like a drinking straw.

83. Click the **Turn cap on for solid appearance** button. The cylinder appears solid, like a pencil.

84. Click the **OK** button to apply the effect.

Copyright Goodheart-Willcox Co., Inc.   For individual use only—reproduction or duplication of this copyrighted material is prohibited.

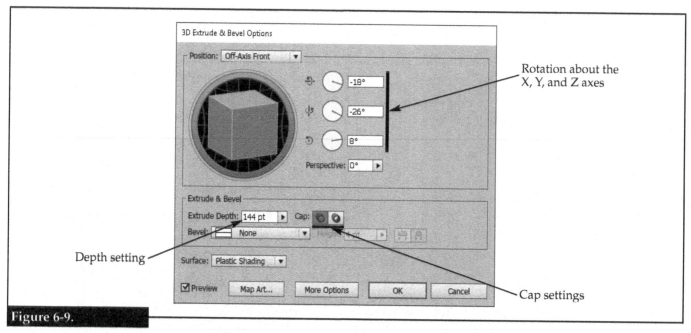

Figure 6-9.

A 3D extrude effect simulates a three-dimensional object, but the shape remains two dimensional.

3D Rotation

As you learned in math class, space has three dimensions each represented by an axis on the Cartesian coordinate system. The three axes are X, Y, and Z. Two-dimensional drawings are created using the X and Y axes. In other words, they are created on the XY plane. The Z axis adds the third dimension needed to create an object with volume. In Illustrator, the position of a two-dimensional shape can be altered to simulate rotation along any of the three axes.

Appearance

TIP
To edit an effect that has been applied, it must be selected from the **Appearance** panel. Otherwise, a second effect will be created and the original effect will be unchanged.

85. With the simulated cylinder selected, click the **Appearance** button in the **Panels** bar to expand the **Appearance** panel.

86. Click the 3D Extrude & Bevel effect in the panel. The **3D Extrude & Bevel Options** dialog box is displayed for modifying the effect. The rotation about the three axes is represented by the three circles and text boxes at the top of the dialog box.

87. Enter 0 in each of the X, Y, and Z rotation text boxes, but do not press the [Enter] key. Notice how the preview shows the circle as flat, but what you are really seeing is the top of the simulated cylinder.

88. Click the rotation wheel for the X axis (top), and drag so the line points up and 90° is displayed in the text box. Notice the circle now appears as a rectangle because you are seeing the side of the simulated cylinder. Its top is now at the top of the screen, so it appears as a line in this view. However, the shape has not changed, only your view of it is different.

89. Change the X rotation to –45 degrees. The X axis runs left to right on the screen, as shown in **Figure 6-10.** It is important to understand the axes are based on the screen, not the shape.

90. Change the Y axis rotation (middle) to 30 degrees. Notice how the effect changes the view of the simulated cylinder.

91. Change the Z axis rotation (bottom) to 120 degrees. Notice the shaded face on the preview cube in the dialog box represents the top of the cylinder.

92. Click the **OK** button to apply the changes to the effect.

For individual use only—reproduction or duplication of this copyrighted material is prohibited.

Copyright Goodheart-Willcox Co., Inc.

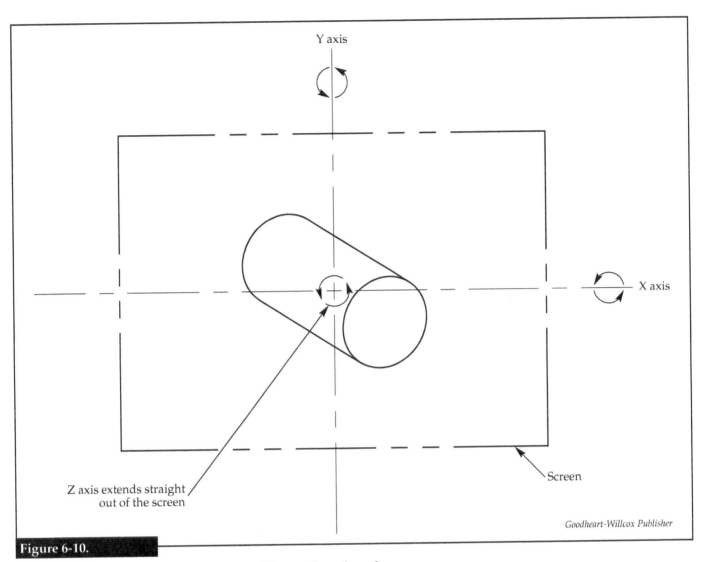

Y axis

X axis

Z axis extends straight
out of the screen

Screen

Goodheart-Willcox Publisher

Figure 6-10.

The axes of rotation for the 3D extrude effect are based on the screen.

Effects Combinations

Effects can be combined to create an end result that cannot be achieved by a single effect. Each effect is displayed in the **Appearance** panel and can be edited.

93. With the simulated cylinder selected, click **Effect>Artistic>Plastic Wrap...** on the **Application** bar. In the **Plastic Wrap** dialog box that is displayed, click the **OK** button to accept all of the default values and apply the effect. Notice how the circle still appears as a simulated cylinder, but now it appears to be wrapped in plastic, like packaging.

94. Click **Effect>Warp>Bulge...** on the **Application** bar. In the **Warp Options** dialog box that is displayed, click the **OK** button to accept all of the default values. Notice this new effect builds on the two previous effects to alter the shape.

95. Applying what you have learned, display the **Appearance** panel.

96. Click the **Toggle Visibility** button (eye) next to the Warp: Bulge entry in the panel. The end result of this effect is hidden on the shape.

97. Click the Plastic Wrap entry in the panel to select it, but do *not* click directly on the name. The name is a link that opens the dialog box for modifying the effect.

For individual use only—reproduction or duplication of this copyrighted material is prohibited.

**Delete
Selected Item**

TIP
The **Appearance** panel allows for changes to all object attributes in one convenient location.

98. With the Plastic Wrap entry selected in the panel, click the **Delete Selected Item** button at the bottom of the panel to permanently remove the effect from the shape.

99. Click the **Toggle Visibility** button next to the Warp: Bulge entry in the panel to make the effect visible. Note that the button is blank when the effect is hidden and displays an eye when the effect is visible.

100. Click the color swatch next to the Fill entry in the **Appearance** panel, and click the drop-down arrow that appears to display color swatches. Click the RGB Red color swatch to change the fill color.

101. Click the **Stroke:** link in the **Appearance** panel. A panel is displayed that can be used to change the stroke properties. Change the stroke weight to 5 points.

102. Click the color swatch next to the **Stroke:** link in the **Appearance** panel, and change the stroke color to RGB Yellow. Notice how the stroke color is used for the depth surfaces of the simulated cylinder.

103. Applying what you have learned, apply a drop shadow Illustrator effect to the volumetric sphere.

104. Save the file, and then click **File>Close** on the **Application** bar to close the document and leave Illustrator open. Close all open documents.

Perspective

A perspective drawing simulates a realistic view by representing receding lines converging at a vanishing point or points, as shown in **Figure 6-11.** The type of perspective drawing is named by the number of vanishing points used in the drawing. Illustrator has powerful tools to simulate a 3D scene using one-, two-, or three-point perspective. Perspective drawing is important in creating realistic graphics.

105. Start a new project named *LastName_*Perspective using the default values for the Art & Illustration profile, and save it in your working folder.

**Perspective
Grid Tool**

106. Click the **Perspective Grid Tool** button in the **Tools** panel. Once this tool is selected, a three-plane perspective grid is placed on the artboard.

107. Draw a rectangle on the artboard. Notice how the rectangle has perspective applied and the top portion is slanted downward, as shown in **Figure 6-12.**

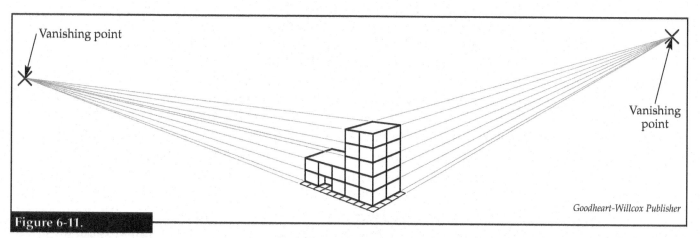

Goodheart-Willcox Publisher

Figure 6-11.

In a perspective drawing, receding lines converge at a vanishing point. The number of vanishing points determines the type of perspective drawing. This is a two-point perspective drawing.

For individual use only—reproduction or duplication of this copyrighted material is prohibited.

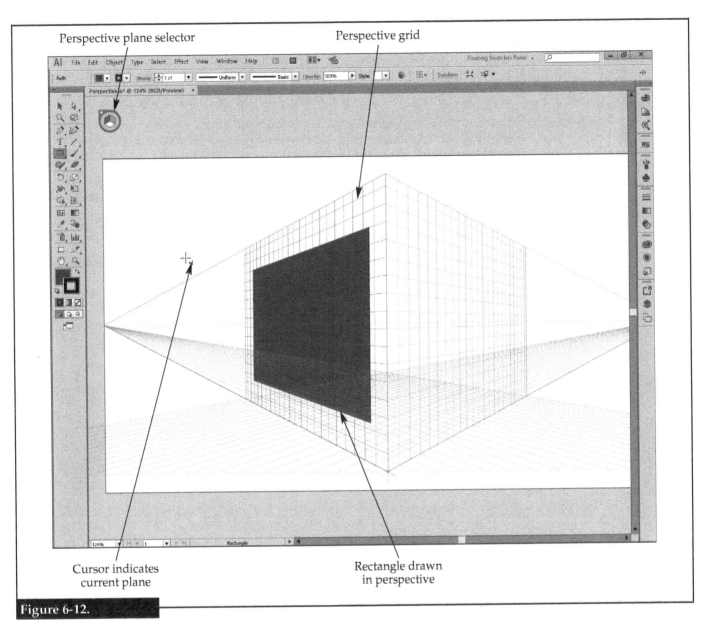

Perspective plane selector

Perspective grid

Cursor indicates current plane

Rectangle drawn in perspective

Figure 6-12.

Illustrator has tools to help create a two-point perspective drawing.

108. Applying what you have learned, change the fill color to RGB Blue, the stroke to black with a weight of 1 point, and transform the rectangle to 300 points wide by 300 points high.

109. Locate the perspective plane selector in the top-left corner of the screen. This is used to change the plane on which a shape will be drawn. A drawing tool must be active to change the drawing plane.

110. With the rectangle tool active, click the dark-gray side of the cube in the perspective plane selector. This face of the cube turns orange to match the orange perspective grid. Also notice the small arrow in the cursor has changed direction.

111. Draw another rectangle object on the right-hand side of artboard.

112. Applying what you have learned, change the fill color to RGB Yellow, the stroke to black with a weight of 1 point, and transform the rectangle to 300 points wide by 300 points high.

Perspective Selection Tool

113. Click **Perspective Selection Tool** button in the **Tools** panel.

Copyright Goodheart-Willcox Co., Inc.

For individual use only—reproduction or duplication of this copyrighted material is prohibited.

TIP

The perspective selection tool must be used to move shapes in perspective mode. If the normal selection tool is used, the proper perspective will not be maintained as the shape is moved.

Type Tool

114. Click the blue rectangle, and drag it around the screen. Notice how Illustrator automatically scales the shape to simulate depth in the scene. See how the shape changes when dragging it upward, downward, forward, and backward.

115. Move the yellow rectangle so that its left-hand edge is at the left-hand edge of the orange grid. Use smart guides to precisely locate the edge.

116. Move the blue rectangle so that its right-hand edge is at the right-hand edge of the blue grid. Also move it up or down as needed so it vertically aligns with the yellow rectangle. You have now created a two-point perspective of a cube, as shown in **Figure 6-13**.

117. Click the **Type Tool** button in the **Tools** panel, and click in the middle of the yellow rectangle.

118. Enter your first and last name.

119. Either use the text tool cursor to highlight the text, or click the **Selection Tool** button in the **Tools** panel to end text editing and select the text box.

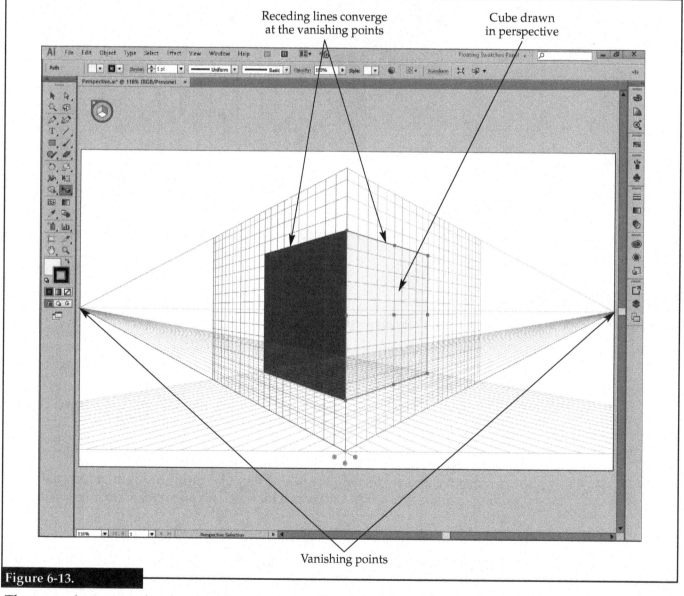

Figure 6-13.

The two-point perspective drawing of a cube is complete. It is composed of two two-dimensional parallelograms that were drawn as rectangles on the perspective grid.

For individual use only—reproduction or duplication of this copyrighted material is prohibited.

Copyright Goodheart-Willcox Co., Inc.

120. Click in the **Font Size:** text box on the **Control** panel, and enter 48. This changes the height of the type to 48 points. Notice at this point the text is not shown in perspective.

121. Click the **Perspective Selection Tool** button, and activate the right-hand grid (orange) perspective in the perspective plane selector.

122. Click and drag your name to the center of the yellow rectangle. The text will automatically align with the perspective grid. Now the text looks like it is written on the yellow face of a cube.

123. Click the **Hide Grid** button (X) on the perspective plane selector. The perspective grid is removed, but the shapes remain drawn in two-point perspective.

124. Save the file.

Proof Options and Exporting

The client wants to see how well 3D objects can be rendered with 2D elements. He wants to see how these will look in both printed materials and on a computer monitor.

125. Applying what you have learned, create a background layer, draw a rectangle that covers the artboard, and fill it with the RGB Magenta color.

126. Click **View>Proof Setup>Working CMYK** on the **Application** bar. The view simulates how the graphic will appear if printed using the four process colors (CMYK). Notice how the colors have shifted drastically from the RGB display. The color luminescence is reduced.

127. Click **View>Proof Setup>Monitor RGB** on the application bar. The view shows the RGB versions of the colors.

128. Click **File>Export>Export As...** on the **Application** bar. To *export* the image is to save it in a format other than the native Adobe Illustrator format. This is typically done to create a format that can be used by other programs. Exporting differs from "save as" in that the file itself is not converted, only a copy of the image is saved in the different format.

129. In the **Export** dialog box, which is a standard save-type dialog box, navigate to your working folder.

130. Click in the **File name:** text box, and enter *LastName*_JPEG.

131. Click the **Save as type:** drop-down arrow, and click **JPEG (*.JPG)** in the drop-down list.

132. Click the **Export** button. A dialog box is displayed for converting the file to a JPEG image.

133. Click the **Color Model:** drop-down arrow, and click **CMYK** in the drop-down list. This setting allows the exported file to be print-ready.

134. Click the **Quality:** drop-down arrow, and click **High** in the drop-down list.

135. Click the **Resolution:** drop-down arrow, and click **High (300 ppi)** in the drop-down list. PPI stands for points or pixels per inch.

136. Click the **OK** button to complete the export as a JPEG file. Notice that the open file in Illustrator is still *LastName*_Perspective.ai. AI is the native format for Illustrator.

137. Applying what you have learned, export the image as a bitmap (BMP) file named *LastName*_BMP in grayscale mode using only screen resolution. If

TIP
An RGB color displayed on a computer monitor is created with projected light, and computer monitors are very bright. A CMYK color printed on paper is created with reflected light, which is not as bright. Also, the RGB color model is additive, where all three colors added together at 100% (value of 255) create white. In the CMYK color model, all four colors added together at 100% create black. The factors combine to produce muted colors in CMYK when compared to RGB.

Copyright Goodheart-Willcox Co., Inc.   For individual use only—reproduction or duplication of this copyrighted material is prohibited.

prompted for additional settings, accept the defaults. A grayscale file is also a print-ready file.

Files for Websites or Mobile Devices

As you saw in the previous section, an Illustrator file can be exported for use in printing. However, the requirements for websites are different from those for printed pieces. Illustrator can easily prepare files for use on a website.

138. Click **File>Export>Export for Screens...** on the **Application** bar. The **Export for Screens** dialog box is displayed, as shown in **Figure 6-14.**

139. Make sure the **Artboards** button is selected (depressed) above the preview area.

140. In the **Select:** area, click the **All** radio button. This will export all artboards.

141. Click the folder icon in the **Export to:** area, browse to your working folder in the dialog box that is displayed, and click the **Select Folder** button to set the save location.

142. In the **Formats:** area of the **Export for Screens** dialog box, click the **iOS** button. This adds presets that are compatible with the iOS to the list of formats. Notice that there are three presets added: 1X, 2X, and 3X.

143. If there is a fourth preset in the list of formats, click the X to the right of the preset to remove it. You should have only the 1X, 2X, and 3X presets.

144. In the list of formats, click the **Format** drop-down arrow for each preset, and click **JPG 100** in the drop-down list. This sets the format to JPEG image format, which is a compressed file type that is suitable for use on websites. The 100 indicates 100% quality setting, which is the highest possible.

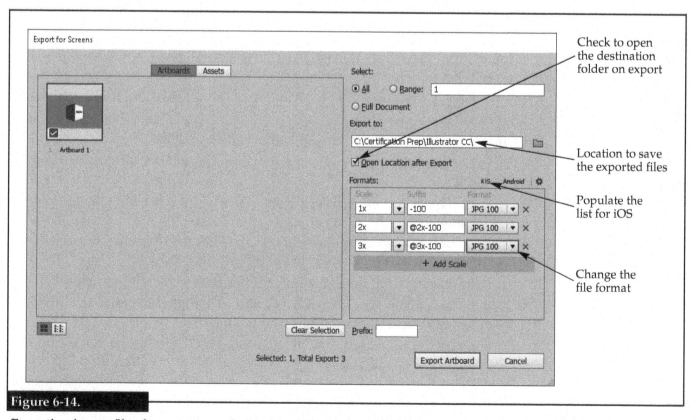

Figure 6-14.

Exporting image files for use on a website or mobile device.

For individual use only—reproduction or duplication of this copyrighted material is prohibited.

Copyright Goodheart-Willcox Co., Inc.

145. Click the **Export Artboard** button to create the three versions of the image as JPEG files.

146. Close Illustrator.

Lesson 6 Review

Vocabulary

In a word processing document or on a sheet of paper, list all of the *key terms* in this lesson. Place each term on a separate line. Then, write a definition for each term using your own words. You will continue to build this terminology dictionary throughout this certification guide.

Review Questions

Answer the following questions. These questions are aligned to questions in the certification exam. Answering these questions will help prepare you to take the exam.

1. Describe how to create a new color swatch in the RGB color group with the values R100, G20, and B200.

_____

_____

_____

_____

_____

2. What is the function of gradient stops?

_____

_____

_____

_____

_____

3. Explain chiaroscuro.

_____

_____

_____

_____

_____

Copyright Goodheart-Willcox Co., Inc.
For individual use only—reproduction or duplication of this copyrighted material is prohibited.

4. What is the function of backlighting?

_____

_____

_____

_____

5. How does a ground shadow help simulate a spatial object?

_____

_____

_____

_____

6. Compare and contrast linear and radial gradients.

_____

_____

_____

_____

_____

7. How is a gradient changed from linear to radial?

_____

_____

_____

_____

8. Describe how to simulate a 4-inch-long cylinder with a circle shape.

_____

_____

_____

_____

9. What are the three axes of the Cartesian coordinate system?

_____

10. Which axis of the Cartesian coordinate system projects straight out of the screen in Illustrator?

_____

11. How can an effect be shown or hidden on a shape after it has been applied?

_____

_____

_____

_____

For individual use only—reproduction or duplication of this copyrighted material is prohibited.   Copyright Goodheart-Willcox Co., Inc.

12. Where must an effect be edited after it has been applied to a shape?

_____

_____

_____

13. Describe a perspective drawing.

_____

_____

_____

_____

14. How is the perspective grid displayed?

_____

_____

15. How is a proof viewed that simulates the four process colors of cyan, magenta, yellow, and black?

_____

_____

_____

_____

16. What is the difference in color models for a proof for printing and a proof for screen display?

_____

_____

_____

_____

17. When exporting a JPEG file from Illustrator, what setting must be made for the file to be print-ready?

_____

_____

_____

_____

18. List the steps needed to export an image as a bitmap in grayscale mode with screen resolution.

_____

_____

_____

_____

  For individual use only—reproduction or duplication of this copyrighted material is prohibited.

19. How is an image saved for a web project?

_____

_____

_____

_____

20. Describe the JPG 100 file format.

_____

_____

_____

_____

For individual use only—reproduction or duplication of this copyrighted material is prohibited.

Copyright Goodheart-Willcox Co., Inc.

Lesson 7
Vector Image Conversion

Objectives

Students will place images in Illustrator. Students will explain the basic process for tracing a bitmap to create a vector image. Students will discuss modification of Bézier curves. Students will create a computer-generated tracing. Students will explain how to crop a photograph using a clipping mask. Students will compare and contrast a standard gradient and a gradient mesh. Students will discuss the purpose of slicing an image. Students will create an opacity mask. Students will interpret copyright information from metadata.

Reading Materials

Adobe Illustrator allows an artist to create original artwork. Many artists choose Illustrator because it is easy to use and it resizes images well. An advantage to using Illustrator is the ability to create and convert art into vector images. Vector images have a small file size and can be resized without loss of quality. When artwork such as a logo needs to be able to be small for a business card or large for a billboard sign, vector art is a great choice. Because of these benefits, sometimes raster images are converted to vector images.

A *copyright* is legal ownership of the work. It protects the creative work by making it illegal for others to copy or use the material without the permission of the owner. As soon as something has been produced in a tangible form, it is automatically copyrighted. This means that if you have an idea for a new character, the idea by itself cannot be copyrighted because an idea is not tangible. You cannot hold, touch, or see an idea. As soon as you draw the character on a sheet of paper, however, that drawing automatically belongs to you and others cannot use it without your permission. The copyright does not need to be registered with the United States Copyright Office, but can be if you choose to do so.

A formal copyright notice consists of the copyright designation, date, and owner. Examples of this include: Copyright 1998 John Smith and ©1998 John Smith. The © symbol means copyright. However, a formal copyright notice or the copyright symbol is not required. Including a notice serves to tell others the work is copyrighted, but if you do not see a notice, you cannot assume the work lacks a copyright. The image or song you find on the Internet most likely is copyrighted. This means you cannot use it unless you get permission from the owner.

According to the *World Intellectual Property Organization (WIPO) Copyright Treaty,* intellectual property, such as music, games, movies, and works of art, is protected worldwide. In the United States, the Digital Millennium Copyright Act (DCMA) enforces the WIPO treaty.

In some limited cases, copyrighted material can be used without the owner's permission under the fair use/fair dealings doctrine. The *fair use/fair dealings doctrine* allows the use of copyrighted material so long as the use is limited to a

 For individual use only—reproduction or duplication of this copyrighted material is prohibited.

description or critique of the work. So a screen capture of a video game used with a description of the game action is not a copyright violation under fair use doctrine. Be aware that the guidelines for claiming usage under fair use/fair dealings doctrine are very strict.

When a creative work has been around for a long time, it is placed in the public domain. *Public domain* applies to any work for which the copyright term has expired. It means any and all copyrights on the work have been removed. There is no more legal protection preventing duplication, and the work is free to use. The time period after which a creative work falls into the public domain varies. For example, in the United States, any work published after 1978 passes into the public domain 70 years after the creator has died.

As a digital artist, it is a best practice to research any image you intend to use to understand what rights are assigned to the image. It is your responsibility to contact the owner and get permission to use any creative work that is not specifically marked as "free use" or "public domain." Be sure to record and save any documentation granting you permission to use the image.

A *trademark* is similar to a copyright, but it is legal ownership of a word, phrase, symbol, or design that identifies the unique source of a product. Designating the logo as trademarked provides legal protection to the design. The ™ symbol indicates that the trademark has not been registered with the United States Patent and Trademark Office. The ® symbol indicates the trademark has been registered.

How to Begin

1. Before beginning this lesson, download the needed files from the student companion website located at www.g-wlearning.com, and unzip them into your working folder. There should be a Client Images folder containing five image files.

2. Launch Adobe Illustrator, and open the **New Document** dialog box to begin setting up a new document.

3. Name the document *LastName*_Tracing, set the number of artboards to 4, and set the size to 640 points wide by 480 points high.

4. Click the triangle next to the **Advanced** label to display the expanded **Advanced** area, as shown in **Figure 7-1.**

5. Click the **Color Mode:** drop-down arrow, and click **RGB** in the drop-down list.

6. Click the **Raster Effects:** drop-down arrow, and click **Screen (72 ppi)** in the drop-down list.

7. Click the **OK** button to create the document.

8. Save the file as *LastName*_Tracing in your working folder.

Place Images

As you saw in the previous lesson, images can be exported from Illustrator. Illustrator can also import images. In Illustrator, importing an image is *placing* it into the drawing. Placing an image allows the designer to add a photograph or other image to the project.

For individual use only—reproduction or duplication of this copyrighted material is prohibited.   Copyright Goodheart-Willcox Co., Inc.

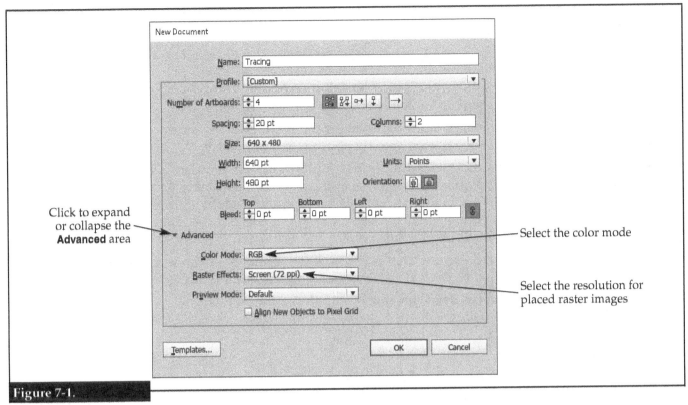

Click to expand
or collapse the
Advanced area

Select the color mode

Select the resolution for
placed raster images

Figure 7-1.

Setting the resolution for raster images placed into the new document.

9. Click **File>Place...** on the **Application** bar. The **Place** dialog box is displayed, which is a standard open-type dialog box.

10. Navigate to your working folder and then the Client Images folder you downloaded earlier.

11. Select the Apple image file, and click the **Place** button. Once the dialog box closes, click on Artboard 1 to place the image there.

12. Click the **Selection Tool** button in the **Tools** panel.

Selection Tool

TIP

In most cases, a placed raster image should not be nonuniformly scaled. To uniformly scale an image using the anchors, hold down the [Shift] key while dragging.

13. Applying what you have learned, use the anchors on the image to resize the image so it exactly fits on the artboard. Notice that this nonuniformly scales the image, so the image is distorted.

14. Click the **Embed** button on the **Control** panel. This breaks the link to the original image file. Until this button is clicked, the original can be edited, and the image in the Illustrator document will be updated to match.

15. Applying what you have learned, place the Pear image on Artboard 2, the Cherries image on Artboard 3, and the Watermelon image on Artboard 4. Resize each to fit the artboard.

Tracing

One reason an artist may place a photograph into an Illustrator document is to trace it to create a vector image. The pen tool allows the artist to draw lines and curves for freehand drawing or to trace the image components on a photograph. This tool is generally the best one for tracing an image because it is flexible and allows both curves and straight lines to be drawn in a single session of the tool.

Pen Tool

TIP

The [Ctrl][+] or [Command][+] key combination can be used to zoom in. The [Ctrl][Spacebar] key combination allows you to draw a box around the area to zoom in. The [Ctrl][–] or [Command][–] key combination can be used to zoom out. The [Spacebar] allows you to click and drag the view around the screen, which is called *panning*.

Direct Selection Tool

Convert anchor points to smooth

16. Use the zoom controls to zoom in on the middle slice in the watermelon image. This will help you better see the image as you trace it.

17. Click the **Pen Tool** button in the **Control** panel, and then single-click at the point on one corner of the watermelon slice. An anchor is placed where you click. Since this was a single-click, the anchor is a corner, not a curve anchor. To create a Bézier-curve anchor, click, hold, and drag.

18. Single-click at the opposite corner. A straight line is drawn across the top of the watermelon slice, and the pen tool remains active.

19. Click, hold, and drag at the middle of the curve on the bottom of the watermelon slice. Notice as you drag that the new line segment is curved instead of straight, as shown in **Figure 7-2.** Release the mouse button to finish placing the anchor. Since three points are the minimum to create a closed shape, the current fill color is applied at this point.

20. Click the first anchor point to close the shape. Do not worry if the shape does not match the watermelon slice. You will edit the curve to match the image.

21. Click the **Selection Tool** button to end the pen tool.

22. Applying what you have learned, change the fill to RGB Green and the stroke to black with a weight of 1 point.

Bézier Modification

As you have seen, anchor points can be drawn as either corners or curves. Once an anchor point is created, it can be converted between the types. Additionally, the shape of curves can be modified and new anchor points can be added to a shape.

23. Click the **Direct Selection Tool** button on the **Tools** panel.

24. Click one of the anchor points at the corner of the watermelon slice. The two anchor points at the corners are currently corner-type points.

25. In the **Control** panel, click the **Convert anchor points to smooth** button. The anchor changes to a curve type, and the corner of the shape is now rounded, which has eliminated the straight line across the top of the watermelon slice. This needs to be corrected.

26. Click the control handle that is on the side of the anchor that should be a straight line segment, and drag and drop the handle directly on top of the anchor. Notice how the straight line segment has been restored, but the other side of the anchor remains a curve, as shown in **Figure 7-3.** This gives you an additional control handle to adjust the curvature of the shape along with the control handles on the anchor that was drawn as a curve type.

27. Applying what you have learned, convert the other corner-type anchor to a smooth-type anchor, and restore the straight line segment.

28. Applying what you have learned, use the control handles on the three anchors to match the shape of the curve to the bottom of the watermelon slice.

29. Applying what you have learned, rename the sublayer for this shape as Rind, and hide it.

30. Applying what you have learned, trace the red fleshy part of the watermelon, fill the shape with RGB Red, and set the stroke to black with a weight of 1 point. Also, rename the sublayer for this shape as Flesh, and hide it.

For individual use only—reproduction or duplication of this copyrighted material is prohibited.

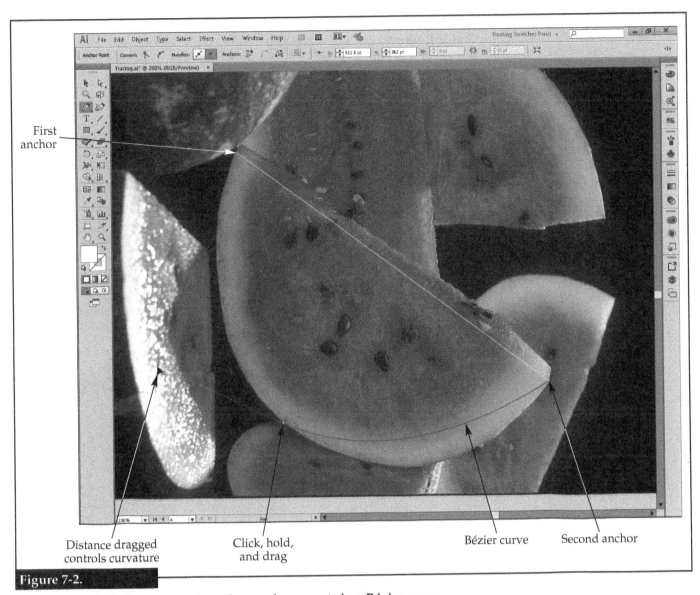

First anchor

Distance dragged controls curvature

Click, hold, and drag

Bézier curve

Second anchor

Figure 7-2.

Creating straight line segments and curved segments in a Bézier curve.

31. Applying what you have learned, draw an ellipse to match the size of one of the watermelon seeds. Just concentrate on the size of the ellipse, not matching the rotation of the seed. Fill the ellipse with black, and set the stroke to None.

32. Click the **Rotate Tool** in the **Tools** panel.

Rotate Tool

33. Click the bottom anchor point of the ellipse, and drag to adjust the rotation until it matches that of the seed.

34. Applying what you have learned, move the ellipse to cover the seed.

35. Click the **Direct Selection Tool** button in the **Tools** panel, and edit the shape of the ellipse to better match the seed.

Direct Selection Tool

36. Applying what you have learned, create four or five more seeds.

37. Applying what you have learned, select and group all of the seed shapes.

38. Applying what you have learned, rename the sublayer for the seeds group as Seeds.

39. Make visible the Flesh and Rind sublayers. Reorder the sublayers if needed to properly build the watermelon slice.

Copyright Goodheart-Willcox Co., Inc.   For individual use only—reproduction or duplication of this copyrighted material is prohibited.

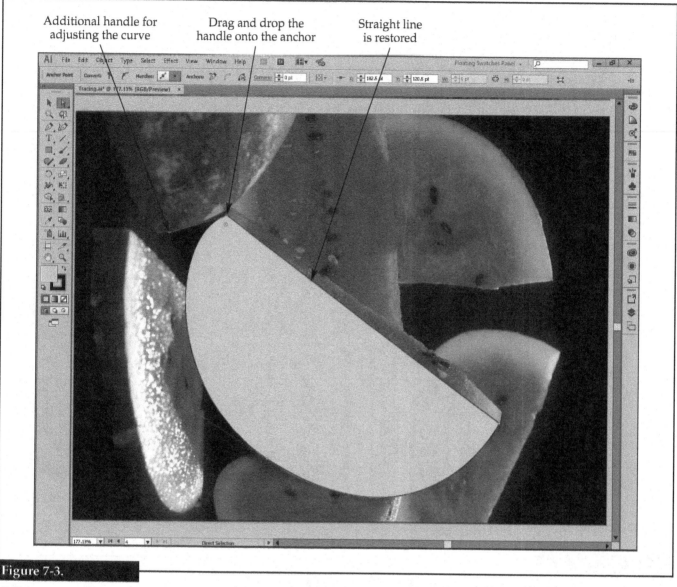

Additional handle for adjusting the curve　　Drag and drop the handle onto the anchor　　Straight line is restored

Figure 7-3.

Editing an anchor point so one side is a curve and the other side is a corner.

Line Segment Tool

40. Click the **Line Segment Tool** in the **Tools** panel. This tool draws only straight line segments. The watermelon slice has thickness, which is currently not represented. A straight line will be added to represent the thickness.

41. Applying what you have learned, set the stroke color to black and the weight to 1 point.

42. Click at one corner of the watermelon, drag to the other corner, and release to draw the straight line segment, as shown in **Figure 7-4.**

43. Applying what you have learned, group all shapes in the watermelon slice as a single object.

44. Move the photograph away from the drawing to compare how well you were able to match the contours and colors of the watermelon slice. Undo the move to return the photograph to its original location.

For individual use only—reproduction or duplication of this copyrighted material is prohibited.

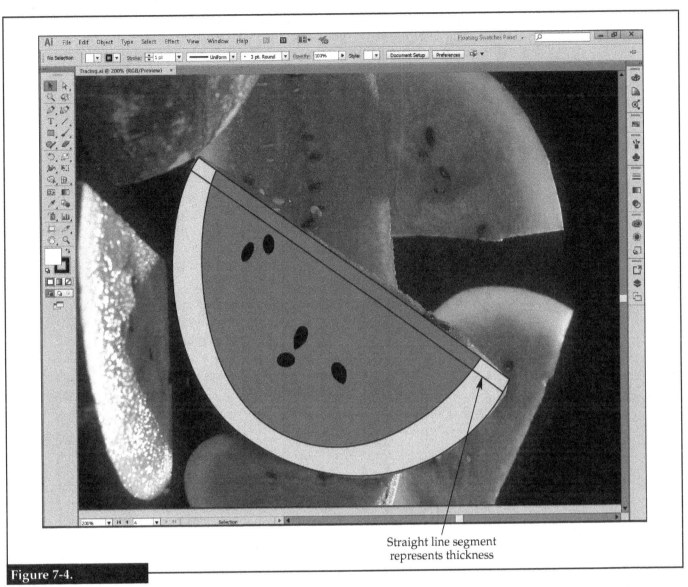

Straight line segment
represents thickness

Figure 7-4.
Adding a straight line segment to give the slice thickness.

Computer-Generated Tracing

As you saw in the previous section, an artist can manually trace a raster image to create vector artwork based on the image. Illustrator can also automatically produce vector artwork by tracing a raster image. In some cases, this produces acceptable results, but in most cases the artist must further edit the vector graphic to fine-tune the artwork.

45. Zoom out as needed, and select the Pear image.

46. Click the drop-down arrow to the right of the **Image Trace** button on the **Control** panel. A drop-down list is displayed containing various options for how to trace the image.

47. Click **3 colors** in the drop-down list. This will convert the image into a vector image using the three most common colors found in the image. The conversion may take a few moments to compute. When it is complete, notice how the various colors in the raster image have been converted to filled shapes. Also notice the **Control** panel has changed to display the **Image Tracing** panel options.

Copyright Goodheart-Willcox Co., Inc.   For individual use only—reproduction or duplication of this copyrighted material is prohibited.

48. Click the **Expand** button on the **Image Tracing** panel on the **Control** panel. All shapes used to build the image are converted to paths. These are shapes filled with one of the three colors Illustrator detected as most commonly occurring in the original image.

49. Applying what you have learned, ungroup the shapes.

50. Select the large purple shape that is the background of the image, and press the [Delete] key to erase it.

51. Remove all purple background shapes. Zoom as needed. There will likely be some small background shapes in the leaves. You can choose to delete these or leave them.

**Direct
Selection Tool**

52. Click the **Direct Selection Tool** button in the **Tools** panel, and select the dark brown shadow shape. Notice how many anchor points are used to create this shape. Also, notice how areas on each pear are shown in shadow. You will now remove the shadow and leaves below the pears, but keep the shadows *on* the pears.

53. Click and drag a selection box around most of the anchor points below the pears, and press the [Delete] key to remove them, as shown in **Figure 7-5**. The remaining shape now needs to be refined to represent the pears.

Some anchors are deleted

Figure 7-5.

The shape that forms the shadows must be modified to remove the ground shadow. First, remove unneeded anchors.

For individual use only—reproduction or duplication of this copyrighted material is prohibited.   Copyright Goodheart-Willcox Co., Inc.

**Delete Anchor
Point Tool**

TIP

It may be useful to convert an anchor point to a corner type and then to a smooth type to display two control handles for the anchor.

54. Applying what you have learned, move anchor points and adjust them as needed to construct the bottom of one pear, as shown in **Figure 7-6.** Notice there are still too many anchor points on the right-hand pear in the illustration.

55. Click the **Delete Anchor Point Tool** button on the **Tools** panel. This tool removes a single anchor point.

56. Click any anchor points that need to be deleted to refine the shape. In general, use as few anchor points as possible, and adjust the shape of the path with the control handles.

57. Applying what you have learned, add and refine anchor points as needed to complete the bottom of the pear.

58. Edit the other pear to construct the bottom on it as well. There may be a white space between the two pears that is actually a shape filled with white. If that is the case, delete the anchor points that define the shape, and adjust the shadow as needed to construct the pear edges.

59. Select all shapes in both pears, and group them.

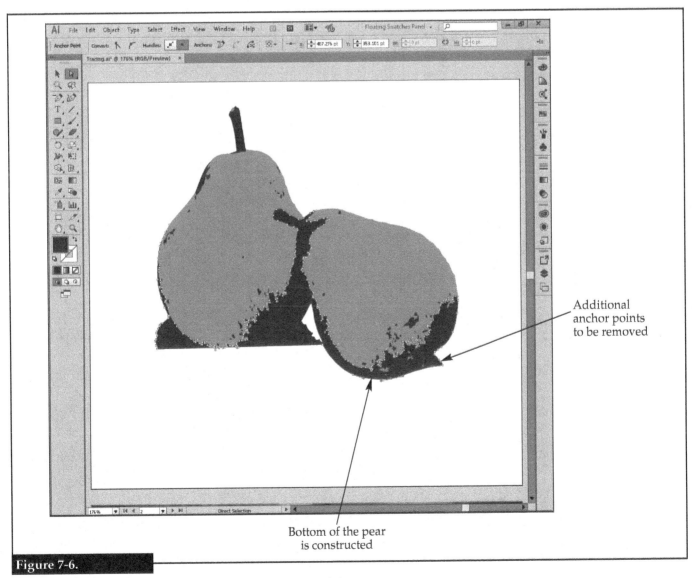

Additional anchor points to be removed

Bottom of the pear is constructed

Figure 7-6.

Refining the shadow shape to match the curvature of the pear.

Copyright Goodheart-Willcox Co., Inc.   For individual use only—reproduction or duplication of this copyrighted material is prohibited.

Masking

TIP

When tracing a raster image, it can be very helpful to set the fill color to None and the stroke to blank with a weight of 1 point. Alternately, set the fill color opacity to 40 percent. This will allow you to see the image while drawing the outline.

Masking is a method of blocking out part of an image using an object or color to specify areas to keep or areas to remove. In this case, you will be using an ellipse shape as a clipping mask to keep an area of an image. A *clipping mask* trims any part of an image that is not covered by the masking. The benefit of using a clipping mask is that it is nondestructive. *Nondestructive* means the original image is unharmed and not permanently altered by the change.

60. Zoom to the Cherries image, and select it. Notice there are two cherries on the left-hand side of the image that are connected by their stems. You will create a clipping mask to isolate these two cherries.

61. Applying what you have learned, trace the two cherries and their stems, as shown in **Figure 7-7.** Draw the basic outline using the pen tool, and then edit the path to refine the shape. Add and delete anchor points as needed.

62. Change the fill color to black and stroke color to None. The fill color can be any color, but black is easy to see against the raster image. You may prefer to use a bright or light color instead.

Mask is created for the cherries →

Figure 7-7.

Two cherries are traced to create a clipping mask. The image outside of the mask will be removed once the mask is applied.

For individual use only—reproduction or duplication of this copyrighted material is prohibited.

Copyright Goodheart-Willcox Co., Inc.

63. Click the **Selection Tool** button on the **Tools** pane, hold down the [Shift] key, and click the raster image and the mask you just created. The objects can be selected in any order, just be sure both are selected.

64. Click **Object>Clipping Mask>Make** on the **Application** bar. The selected items are combined to create the clipping mask. The entire image is hidden except for the two cherries covered by the shape you created.

Gradient Mesh

A *mesh* is a like a net that is placed over an object. *Mesh points* are formed where the mesh lines intersect. A *gradient mesh* is a special type of gradient in which color transitions from one mesh point to the next closest mesh point. It can be thought of as a two-dimensional color transition as opposed to a one-dimensional color transition found in a standard gradient.

65. Zoom as needed so the Apple image fills the screen.

66. Draw an ellipse that approximately matches the shape of the apple in the background. Fill it with black and change the stroke to None.

67. Applying what you have learned, change the opacity to 40 percent. This will allow you to see the apple image while fine-tuning the shape.

68. Applying what you have learned, fine-tune the shape to match the apple. Add or remove anchor points as needed.

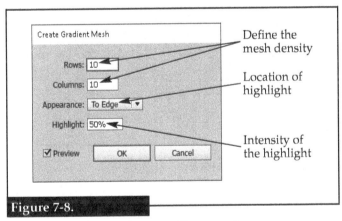

Figure 7-8.

Defining the mesh for a gradient mesh.

69. Change the fill color of the shape to RGB Red and the opacity to 30 percent.

70. Click **Object>Create Gradient Mesh...** on the **Application** bar. The **Create Gradient Mesh** dialog box is displayed, as shown in **Figure 7-8**.

71. Click in the **Rows:** text box, and enter 10.

72. Click in the **Columns:** text box, and enter 10. The rows and columns define the density of the mesh applied over the tracing.

73. Click the **Appearance:** drop-down arrow, and click **To Edge** in the drop-down list. This sets how the highlight will be applied.

74. Click in the **Highlight:** text box, and enter 50%. This is the intensity of the light source.

75. Click the **OK** button to create the mesh. With the semitransparent mesh in place, it is easy to find the specular highlight, diffuse color, and ambient color of the apple. The gradient mesh will allow you to place a gradient at each mesh point to blend these color elements into your tracing.

76. Locate the specular highlight on the apple. This is the white area on the top of the apple. There are several mesh points that need to be blended with white to recreate the specular highlight of the apple. Each mesh point is an anchor point and can be adjusted just as if the mesh were a shape.

77. Using the direct selection tool, click one of the mesh points around the specular highlight and drag it closer to the center of the highlight.

78. Drag the other mesh points around the highlight so they are inside the specular highlight of the original apple, as shown in **Figure 7-9**. There should be about nine mesh points that need to be moved.

Copyright Goodheart-Willcox Co., Inc.   For individual use only—reproduction or duplication of this copyrighted material is prohibited.

Mesh points are moved
inside the specular highlight

Figure 7-9.

Move the mesh points that are near the specular highlight so the points are within the highlight.

Recolor Artwork

79. Select one of the mesh points you moved inside the specular highlight. The selected mesh point will be blue, and all other points will be white.

80. Click the **Recolor Artwork** button on the **Control** panel. The **Recolor Artwork** dialog box is displayed, as shown in **Figure 7-10.** This dialog box allows you to replace the existing color at the selected mesh point with a new color. The new color will be blended with the surrounding colors using a gradient.

81. Click in the **S** text box, and change the value to 10. A saturation setting of 10 percent removes most of the red in the color. As a result, the color is mostly white.

82. Make sure the **Recolor Art** check box is checked. This specifies that the color will be changed for the selected mesh point.

83. Click the **OK** button to apply the new color to the mesh point. Since the opacity of the shape is low, the color change may not be apparent, but this will be corrected later.

84. Applying what you have learned, change the color of all mesh points for the specular highlight of the apple.

For individual use only—reproduction or duplication of this copyrighted material is prohibited.

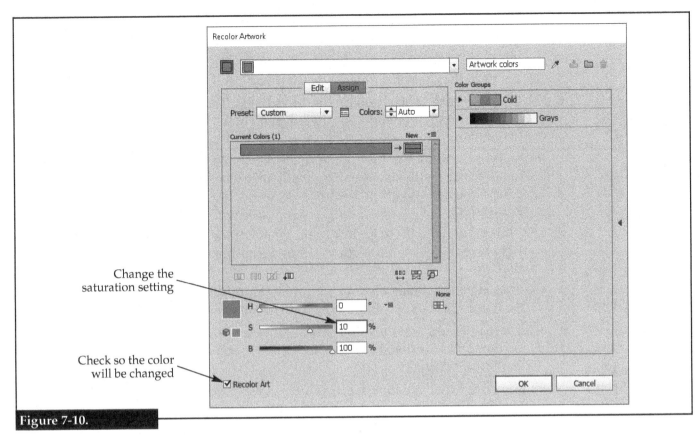

Figure 7-10.

Recoloring a point in a gradient mesh.

Change the saturation setting

Check so the color will be changed

85. Select the darkest mesh point nearest to the bottom center of the apple. Due to the curvature of the apple, this area is shaded from the light source and the color is darker. This is the ambient color of the apple.

86. Hold down the [Shift] key, and select the other mesh points along the bottom that are in the ambient color.

87. Applying what you have learned, recolor the selected mesh points by lowering the brightness setting (**B**) to 25 percent.

88. Make any additional adjustments needed to recolor the gradient mesh to best match the original apple. The shading does not need to be perfect. Imperfections often add authenticity to natural objects. Nature is rarely perfect.

89. Click the **Selection Tool** button on the **Tools** panel, and click the tracing object to select it. The object needs to be clicked even if it appears to be selected in order to fully select it.

90. Applying what you have learned, change the opacity of the tracing object from 30 percent to 100 percent. The vector shape of the apple is fully visible.

TIP

Clicking in the area between four mesh points automatically selects those four points. This can help to quickly select a large number of mesh points. Be careful, though, to make sure previously selected points are not deselected.

Slicing

Slicing in Illustrator is breaking up an image into rectangular sections called tiles. Each tile contains a smaller portion of the full image. The purpose of slicing is to reduce the amount of time it takes for an image to be displayed on a website. Each slice of the image is a small file and can be quickly displayed. The full image will be a much larger file and would take longer to be displayed on a website.

Copyright Goodheart-Willcox Co., Inc.   For individual use only—reproduction or duplication of this copyrighted material is prohibited.

Slice Tool

91. Applying what you have learned, add a new artboard below Artboard 4, place the Grapefruit image file on the artboard, and nonproportionally resize the image to fill the artboard. Embed the image.

92. Zoom so the Grapefruit image fills the screen, and select the image.

93. Click the **Slice Tool** button on the **Tools** panel. The slice tool will allow you to draw in rectangular cuts over the image to make tiles as individual images of the main image.

94. Start in the top-left corner of the Grapefruit image, and drag to the center point. Smart guides will not appear. You will have to estimate the center. When you release the mouse button, the image is sliced into three parts, as shown in **Figure 7-11.**

95. With the slice tool active, click in the center of the image, and drag to the lower-right corner. This splits Section 2 into two additional tiles for a total of four tiles.

Slice Selection Tool

TIP

If the edges of a slice need to be edited, click the **Direct Selection Tool** button in the **Tools** panel, and adjust the edges as needed.

96. Click the **Slice Selection Tool** button on the **Tools** panel, and click inside Section 1. The border of the section turns blue to indicate it is selected.

97. Try to select each of the other three sections. Notice that you can only select Section 1 and Section 4 as these are the two sections you drew. Sections 2 and 3 cannot be selected.

98. Applying what you have learned, draw slices to match Section 3 and Section 4. You should now have four selectable sections.

99. Select all four slices. Either hold down the [Shift] key and select each one or draw a selection box around all four.

100. Click **File>Save Selected Slices...** on the **Application** bar. A standard save-type dialog box is displayed.

101. Click in the **File name:** text box, and enter *LastName*_Slices.

102. Click the **Save as type:** drop-down arrow. Notice the only available file type is GIF.

103. Click the **Save** button to save the slices as separate image files.

104. Using the system file explorer, open your working folder. Notice a subfolder named images was automatically created. Within this subfolder, each slice is a separate image file with the name *LastName*_Slices and a sequential number. These images can be assembled in the programming for a website to display as a single image even though there are four separate files.

Opacity Mask

105. Applying what you have learned, add the text GRAPEFRUIT over the grapefruit photograph.

106. Set the text fill to white with no outline, and set the size to 72 points. Select a sans serif typeface, and set it to bold.

107. Center the text over the glass at the bottom of the grapefruit photograph.

108. Select the text and the grapefruit photograph.

Transparency

109. Click the **Transparency** button in the **Panels** bar to display the **Transparency** panel.

110. Click the **Make Mask** button in the **Transparency** panel. The letters appear to be filled with the photograph. What is happening is the white areas of the text

For individual use only—reproduction or duplication of this copyrighted material is prohibited.

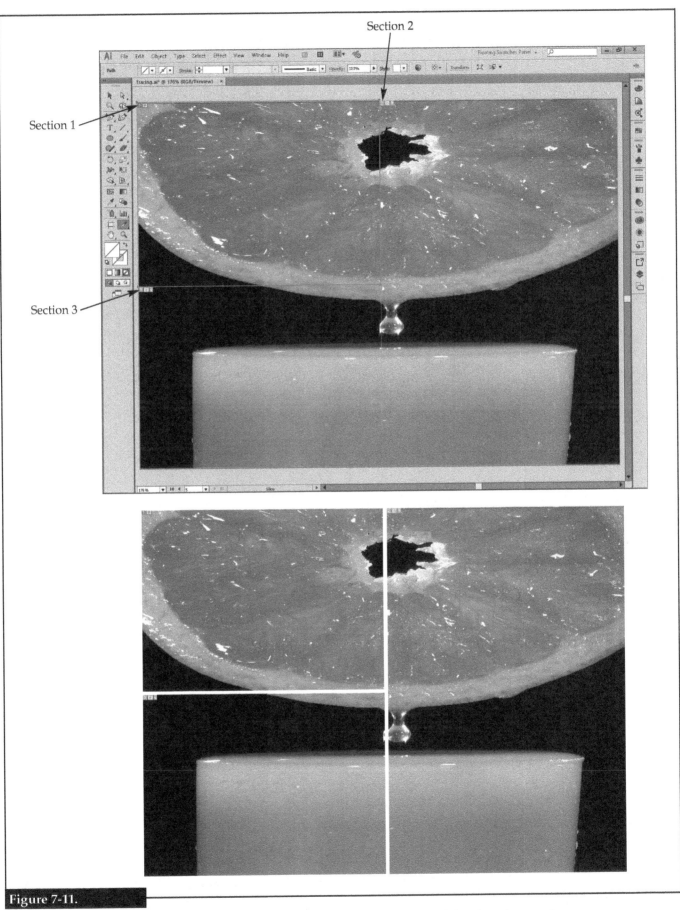

Figure 7-11.

Slicing an image. Only Section 1 is selectable. New slices must be created for the other sections.

Copyright Goodheart-Willcox Co., Inc. For individual use only—reproduction or duplication of this copyrighted material is prohibited.

specify which part of the image to keep. In a transparency mask, black blocks the image and white allows the image to be seen.

111. Click the **Release** button in the **Transparency** panel. The transparency mask is removed, and the objects are no longer locked together.

Copyrights

To help protect your work and designate your copyright, metadata can be embedded into the image file. *Metadata* are information about the file, not part of the main content. This can include copyright and authorship information.

112. Click **File>File Info...** on the **Application** bar. A dialog box for entering metadata is displayed.

113. Click **Basic** on the left of the dialog box, and then edit the information to include your name, the subject of the file, and keywords that can be used to search for the file, as shown in **Figure 7-12**.

114. Click the **Copyright Status:** drop-down arrow, and click **Copyrighted** in the drop-down list.

115. Click in the **Copyright Notice:** text box, and enter an appropriate copyright statement.

116. Click the **OK** button to save the information.

117. Save the file, and close Illustrator.

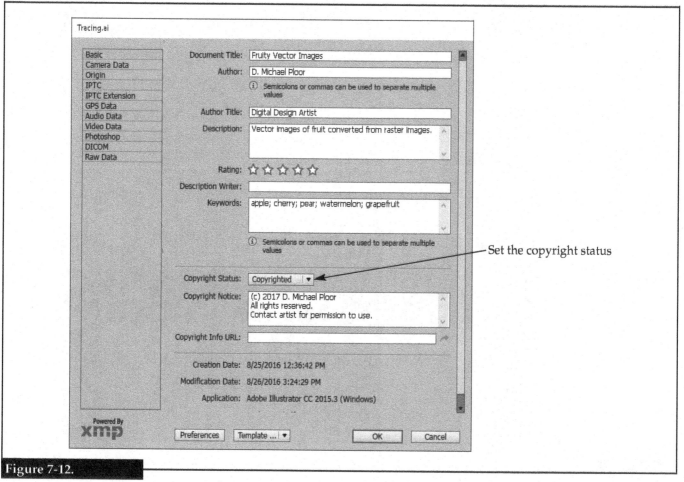

Figure 7-12.

Adding metadata to the Illustrator document.

For individual use only—reproduction or duplication of this copyrighted material is prohibited.

Lesson 7 Review

Vocabulary

In a word processing document or on a sheet of paper, list all of the *key terms* in this lesson. Place each term on a separate line. Then, write a definition for each term using your own words. You will continue to build this terminology dictionary throughout this certification guide.

Review Questions

Answer the following questions. These questions are aligned to questions in the certification exam. Answering these questions will help prepare you to take the exam.

1. What is the process of importing an image into Illustrator called?

2. Which tool is best for tracing a bitmap image by hand? Why?

3. Describe how to convert a curve-type anchor point to a corner-type anchor point.

4. After selecting a raster image on the artboard, what steps are needed to create a computer-generated tracing using only the tools found on the **Image Tracing** panel on the **Control** panel?

5. Describe how to use a clipping mask to have only the portion of a placed photograph that is directly under a star shape be visible.

For individual use only—reproduction or duplication of this copyrighted material is prohibited.

6. How does a gradient mesh compare to a standard gradient?

_____

_____

_____

_____

7. How is a mesh point moved?

_____

_____

_____

_____

8. Why would an image be divided using the slice tool?

_____

_____

_____

_____

9. When does a creative work gain copyright protection?

_____

_____

_____

_____

10. What does it mean if the metadata marks the file as public domain?

_____

_____

_____

_____

For individual use only—reproduction or duplication of this copyrighted material is prohibited.

Lesson 8
Text and Templates

Objectives

Students will discuss the use of placeholder text. Students will compare and contrast kerning and tracking character spacing. Students will explain converting text to curves (outlines). Students will apply text wrapping to an image. Students will apply a graphic style. Students will identify printer marks. Students will employ brush libraries. Students will describe fitting text to a path. Students will create a template file. Students will explain why an Illustrator document would be packaged.

Situation

The Nocturnal Interactive Computer Entertainment (NICE) company is beginning to consider producing marketing pieces for its video games. It wants to have a template that can be used as a consistent starting point for all brochures. To prove you have the skills needed to take on the task of developing the company templates, you have been asked to create a template for a marketing brochure for the owner's side business of fruit grower.

How to Begin

1. Launch Adobe Illustrator.

2. Click **File>New from Template...** on the **Application** bar. The **New from Template** dialog box is displayed, which is a standard open-type dialog box used for selecting a template file. The current folder should be the default templates folder for Illustrator. If not, navigate to the folder containing the Illustrator templates. A *template* is an existing document that has already been formatted, but needs to be customized with content.

3. Open the Blank Templates folder to see the templates available in that category. Note: due to the continuous updates for Creative Cloud, the templates and folders on your system may differ from the ones discussed in this certification guide.

4. Select the Brochure.ait template file, and click the **New** button. A new document is started based on this template. In this case, there are two artboards on the canvas that have guidelines applied to create the front and back of a trifold brochure.

5. Click **Edit>Color Settings...** on the **Application** bar.

6. Click the **Settings:** drop-down arrow, and click **North America Prepress 2** in the drop-down list. This setting tells Illustrator to use a color space that emulates how the colors will appear when the document is printed on a printing press.

7. Click the **OK** button to apply the settings.

8. Save the file as a *document* named *LastName*_Brochure in your working folder. Make sure the file type is a document (.ai), not a template (.ait). While creating the template, you will be working in an Illustrator document file. Later you will

TIP
The [Ctrl][Shift][N] key combination can be used to quickly display the **New from Template** dialog box.

TIP
Notice that the document name is Untitled. When you start a document based on a template, you are not *opening* the template file.

Copyright Goodheart-Willcox Co., Inc.   For individual use only—reproduction or duplication of this copyrighted material is prohibited.

save this document as a template file. Accept all default settings in the **Illustrator Options** dialog box.

Placeholder Text

In Illustrator, text is held in a **text box**. A text box can be moved and resized to fit the size of text and layout requirements. Placeholder text is used in a template to show the user where text should be entered. Often, the placeholder text is Greeked, which means it is dummy text that is not composed of real English words. This is also commonly referred to as *Lorem Ipsum* as those are the two "words" that usually appear at the beginning of the dummy text. The purpose of Greeked text is to have reviewers focus on the design instead of reading the words on the page. In the case of a template, Greeked text is also used to identify text that needs to be replaced with real or live copy (text). In some cases, placeholder text in a template is intended to be used as is without alteration. For example, a company's name and address may be included in a template to ensure it always appears the same across all brochures. In this case, the placeholder text is called *boilerplate* copy.

9. Click the **Artboard Tool** button in the **Tools** panel. Notice that the left-hand artboard is named Brochure Outside and the right-hand artboard is named Brochure Inside. Think of these two artboards as the two sides of a sheet of paper. The paper will be folded on the guidelines to create a three-panel brochure. One side of the paper becomes the inside of the brochure, while the other side of the paper becomes the outside.

10. Press the [Esc] key to exit editing the artboards.

11. Click the **Type Tool** button in the **Tools** panel, and click and drag to create a text box that spans the middle panel near the bottom on the Brochure Outside artboard. Use smart guides to locate the edges of the text box on the vertical guidelines.

12. Enter the text: 123 Orchard Avenue, Fruitville, Florida 00456, p. 800-555-1234, f. 800-555-5678. This is boilerplate copy that will be included in the template.

13. Zoom in on the text box.

14. Click the **Selection Tool** button in the **Tools** panel, and then click the text box to select it.

15. Click the **Set the font family** drop-down arrow on the **Control** panel, and click **Times New Roman** in the drop-down list. Illustrator calls a typeface a font family. If this typeface is not installed on your computer, select any serif typeface.

16. Click the **Font Size** drop-down arrow on the **Control Panel**, and click **10 pt** in the drop-down list.

17. Click the **Paragraph** link on the **Control** panel, and click the **Align Center** button in the panel that is displayed, as shown in **Figure 8-1**. The text is center aligned in the text box.

18. Click the **Type Tool** button in the **Tools** panel, and click to the left of the p in p. 800. This places the cursor in that location for text editing.

19. Press the [Backspace] key twice to delete the space and the comma, and then press the [Enter] key to break the line of text. The phone number and fax number are now on a second line.

20. Applying what you have learned, edit the text so the fax number is on a third line.

Type Tool

Selection Tool

TIP

If resized text is too large to fit the text box, the text box is not automatically resized to fit the text. A red plus sign at the lower-right corner of the text box indicates overflow text. *Overflow* occurs when the text box contains more text than is displayed.

Align Center

For individual use only—reproduction or duplication of this copyrighted material is prohibited.

Copyright Goodheart-Willcox Co., Inc.

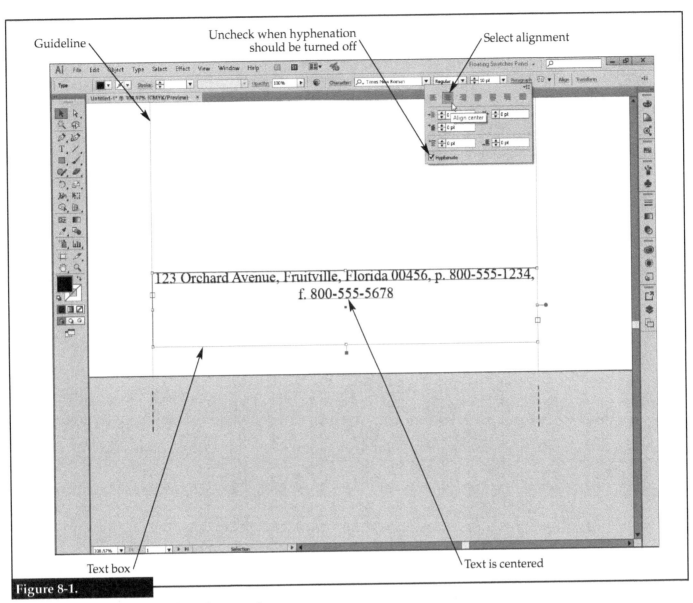

Figure 8-1.

Changing the alignment of text in a text box.

Character Spacing

The kerning and tracking change the spacing of the characters, as shown in **Figure 8-2**. *Kerning* is the spacing between pairs of letters, such as A and V. *Tracking* is the spacing between all characters.

21. Applying what you have learned, add a text box and the text VALLEY FRUIT GROWERS (in all capital letters) to the right-hand panel on the Brochure Outside artboard. This panel is the front of the brochure.

22. Center the text on the panel, change the typeface (font family) to Arial or other sans serif typeface, change the font style to black, and change the size to 36 points.

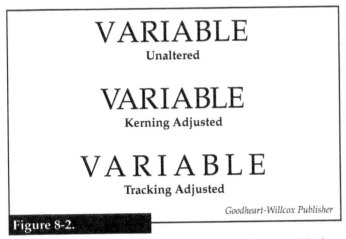

Goodheart-Willcox Publisher

Figure 8-2.

Kerning is the spacing between pairs of letters. Notice the positions of the V and the A. Tracking is the spacing between all characters.

Copyright Goodheart-Willcox Co., Inc.   For individual use only—reproduction or duplication of this copyrighted material is prohibited.

23. Select the text box, and click the **Paragraph** link in the **Control** panel. In the panel that is displayed, uncheck the **Hyphenate** check box. This suppresses hyphenation for the copy in the text box.

24. If a red plus sign appears at the lower-right corner of the text box indicating overflow copy, click and drag the bottom handle of the text box to resize it until all of the copy is visible.

25. Switch to the type tool, and click between the V and A in the word *valley*. Pay attention to the positions of the letters A and V in relation to each other.

26. Click the **Character** link in the **Control** panel. In the panel that is displayed, notice the kerning is set to –57, as shown in **Figure 8-3**. Note: this value may be different if you selected a different typeface.

27. Click the kerning text box in the panel, and enter –225. Notice how the letters are now very close together and almost touching.

28. Applying what you have learned, change the kerning for the letters V and A to 200. Notice how the letters are moved farther apart.

29. Applying what you have learned, change the kerning for the letters V and A to Auto.

TIP

To enter a value for kerning, the cursor must be between two letters. If the letters are selected, you can only select a preset kerning setting, such as Auto.

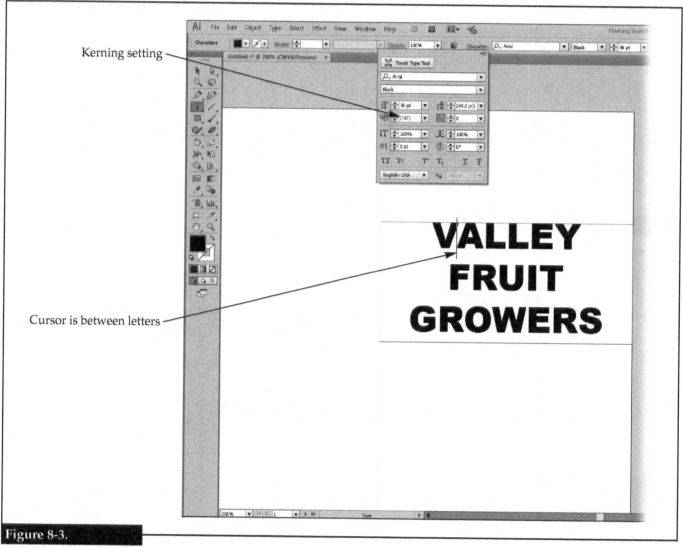

Kerning setting

Cursor is between letters

VALLEY FRUIT GROWERS

Figure 8-3.

Adjusting the kerning between the letters V and A.

For individual use only—reproduction or duplication of this copyrighted material is prohibited.   Copyright Goodheart-Willcox Co., Inc.

Swatches

30. Applying what you have learned, display the **Swatches** panel. Notice there are no swatches displayed. This is because the swatches are saved with the file, and this template does not have any swatches saved in it.

31. Click the **Swatch Libraries Menu** drop-down arrow at the bottom of the **Swatches** panel, and then click **Default Swatches>Art & Illustration** in the drop-down menu. The **Art & Illustration** swatches panel is displayed as a floating panel.

32. Click the **Type Tool** button on the **Tools** panel, and double-click the word *valley*. The word is selected (highlighted).

33. Use the **Art & Illustration** swatches panel to assign the color RGB Green to the selected text.

34. Applying what you have learned, change the color of the word *fruit* to RGB Red and the color of the word *growers* to RGB Yellow.

35. Applying what you have learned, select the text box on the front of the brochure.

36. Click the **Character** link on the **Control** panel.

37. In the panel that is displayed, click in the leading text box, and enter 50. Notice how the lines of text are farther apart, as shown in **Figure 8-4.** *Leading* (pronounced *led-ing*) is the vertical space between the lines. It is measured from

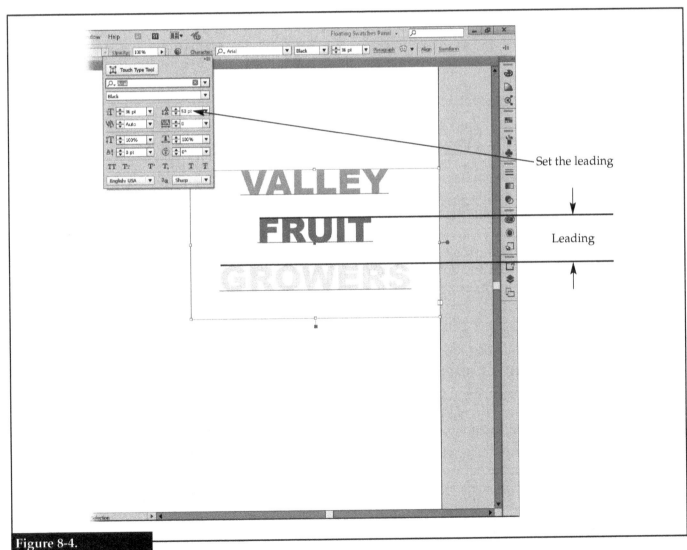

Figure 8-4.

Leading is the vertical spacing between lines, but the measure includes the height of characters.

Copyright Goodheart-Willcox Co., Inc.   For individual use only—reproduction or duplication of this copyrighted material is prohibited.

the top of an uppercase letter in one line to the top of an uppercase letter in the next line.

38. If needed, change the size of the text box so all of the text is visible.

Convert Text to Vector

Many times an illustrator will want to change the shape of letters to create an artistic or stylized effect. However, the characters in a typeface cannot be edited in that way unless the text is converted into a vector graphic. This process is commonly called *converting to curves*. In Illustrator, it is called *creating outlines*. Once converted to curves or outlines, the characters can be modified just like any other vector graphic.

39. Applying what you have learned, select the text box on the front of the brochure.

40. Click **Type>Outlines** on the **Application** bar. Each letter is converted into a vector graphic. The outer edge of each letter is the path containing the fill color.

Direct Selection Tool

41. Click the **Direct Selection Tool** button on the **Tools** panel. The anchors are displayed on each letter. Remember, at this point, the text is no longer type, it is vector graphics.

42. Zoom in on the V in the word *valley*.

43. Applying what you have learned, edit the top of the V to a form of your own design, as shown in **Figure 8-5**. For example, you may choose to make the top look like the peaks of a mountain to stylize the V as a valley since the word is *valley*.

44. Modify the first letter in the words *fruit* and *growers* to be stylized.

Text Wrap

A common illustrative technique, especially in sales brochures, is to place an image within a block of copy. The copy flows, or wraps, around the image. Illustrator has a function to easily allow this.

45. Launch an Internet browser, and search for Greeked text generator. Select a site that is free to use, and copy the Greeked text. Alternately, you can copy any text from any document you may have, such as a report. There should be enough text to completely fill one panel on the brochure you are creating in Illustrator.

46. Switch to Illustrator.

47. Applying what you have learned, draw a text box that completely fills the middle panel on the Brochure Inside artboard.

48. Click **Edit>Paste** on the **Application** bar to insert the Greeked text into the text box.

49. Applying what you have learned, format the text as Times New Roman (or any serif typeface), 11 points in size, 13 points in leading, and justified with the last line aligned left.

50. Applying what you have learned, resize the text box so there is 36 points of space between all sides and the borders of the middle panel. The positions do not have to be exact, and it is okay if there is overflow text in the text box that is not visible.

TIP
Display the ruler to provide a visual cue to the amount of space around the text box.

51. Open the *LastName_*Tracing file created in the last lesson.

52. Select the watermelon slice vector graphic you created, and group the shapes.

For individual use only—reproduction or duplication of this copyrighted material is prohibited.

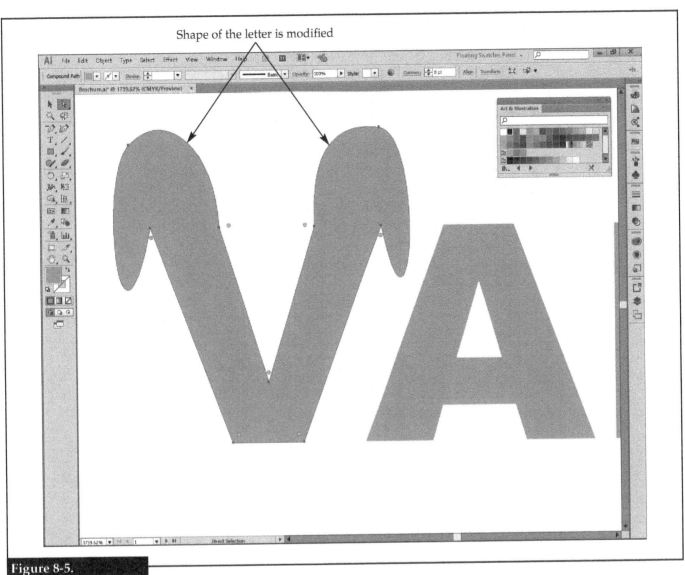

Shape of the letter is modified

Figure 8-5.
After text has been converted to curves (outlines), the characters can be modified just like any other vector shape.

53. Copy the watermelon slice, and then close the file without saving it.

54. Paste the slice into the brochure file, and move it to the center of the middle panel on the Brochure Inside artboard.

55. Applying what you have learned, uniformly scale the watermelon slice so it is about half the width of the text box. If needed, move the group back to the center of the panel.

56. Click **Object>Text Wrap>Make** on the **Application** bar. The text now wraps around the watermelon slice.

57. Move the watermelon slice to the right-hand side of the text box. Notice how the text rewraps.

58. With the watermelon slice selected, click **Object>Text Wrap>Text Wrap Options...** on the **Application** bar.

59. In the **Text Wrap Options** dialog box, check the **Preview** check box.

TIP
If the text does not wrap, be sure the shape around which it should wrap is at the top of the sublayer stack in the **Layers** panel.

Copyright Goodheart-Willcox Co., Inc. For individual use only—reproduction or duplication of this copyrighted material is prohibited.

60. Click in the **Offset:** text box, and enter 15 pt. This sets the distance that will be the buffer between the shape and the text. Notice how the text now wraps around the shape, as shown in **Figure 8-6.**

61. Click the **OK** button to update the setting.

Graphic Styles

A *graphic style* is a fill and stroke pattern that can be quickly added to a group of selected items. Using graphic styles is an easy way to provide a unified look to a document.

62. On the Brochure Inside artboard, add the text Fruit Facts to the first page (left-hand panel). Select a sans serif typeface, and set the size to 48 points.

63. Click the **Graphic Styles** button in the **Panel** bar.

Graphic Styles

64. Applying what you have learned, select the Artistic Effects library in the **Graphic Styles** panel.

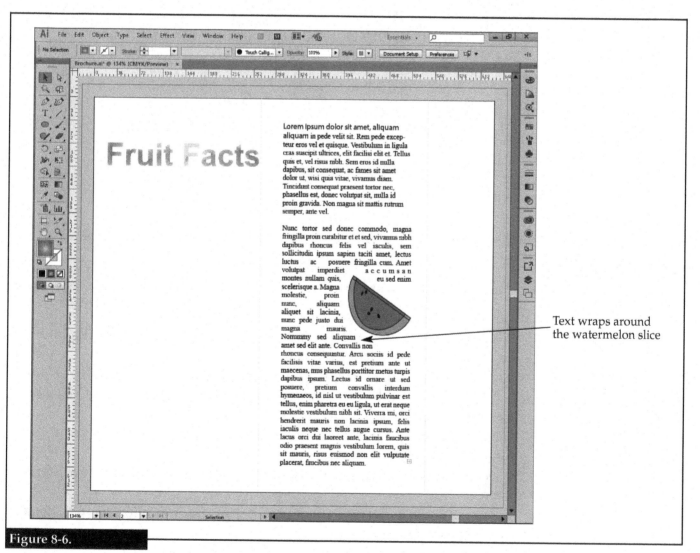

Text wraps around the watermelon slice

Figure 8-6.

When text wrapping is applied to a graphic, any text on a layer below it will flow around the graphic.

For individual use only—reproduction or duplication of this copyrighted material is prohibited.

Copyright Goodheart-Willcox Co., Inc.

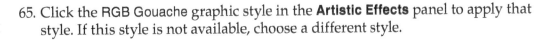

65. Click the RGB Gouache graphic style in the **Artistic Effects** panel to apply that style. If this style is not available, choose a different style.

Printer Marks

Printer marks provide information to the printer, such as showing the printer where to trim and fold the printed sheet. The brochure template includes fold lines that are outside of each artboard above and below the guidelines. These indicate where the printed sheet should be folded. The actual printed piece will be printed on an oversize sheet so these marks are visible and then trimmed to the final size. Trim lines should also be added.

66. Click **File>Document Setup** on the **Application** bar. The **Document Setup** dialog box is displayed.

67. Applying what you have learned, set the bleed to 20 points on all sides.

68. Applying what you have learned, draw a rectangle that extends to all bleed lines on the Brochure Outside artboard.

69. Fill the rectangle with a light orange color of your choice.

70. Rearrange the sublayers so the rectangle is at the bottom. The text on the middle and front panels should be visible.

71. Click the **Artboard Tool** button in the **Tools** panel. Notice trim lines appear at the corners of the active artboard. These are automatically added to each artboard.

72. Click **File>Print...** on the **Application** bar. The **Print** dialog box is displayed.

73. Click **Marks and Bleed** on the left of the dialog box, as shown in **Figure 8-7.**

74. In the **Marks** area, check the **Trim Marks** check box.

75. Click the **Trim Mark Weight:** drop-down arrow, and click **0.25 pt** in the drop-down list.

76. Click in the **Offset:** text box, and enter 25. This value should be greater than the bleed value.

77. If you have access to a printer that can print 11" × 17" sheets, click the **Print** button. Otherwise, click the **Done** button. The trim marks are outside of the printable area for an 8 1/2" × 11" sheet.

Brush Libraries

Brush libraries contain brush tips that change the shape of the stroke applied with the paintbrush tool. By using different brushes, a wide variety of strokes can be created.

78. Double-click the **Paintbrush Tool** on the **Tools** panel. The **Paintbrush Tool Options** dialog box is displayed.

79. Click the **Fidelity** slider, and drag it to the center stop. This will take away sharp points that are drawn and make the points into curves.

80. Make sure the **Edit Selected Paths** check box is checked, and enter 10 in the **Within:** text box. This setting will make the line drawn less precise and more even. Any squiggly parts of the brush stroke will be converted to straight lines and curves when the sides of the line are less than 10 pixels apart.

81. Click the **OK** button to close the dialog box and activate the tool.

82. Applying what you have learned, expand the **Brushes** panel.

TIP
A color theme can be applied in the same way as a graphic style, but color themes must be first created and saved to your Adobe cloud account. To apply a theme, click the **Color** button in the **Panels** bar, and then click the **Color Themes** tab to display the **Color Themes** panel. The available color themes are displayed in this panel.

Artboard Tool

Paintbrush Tool

Brushes

Copyright Goodheart-Willcox Co., Inc. For individual use only—reproduction or duplication of this copyrighted material is prohibited.

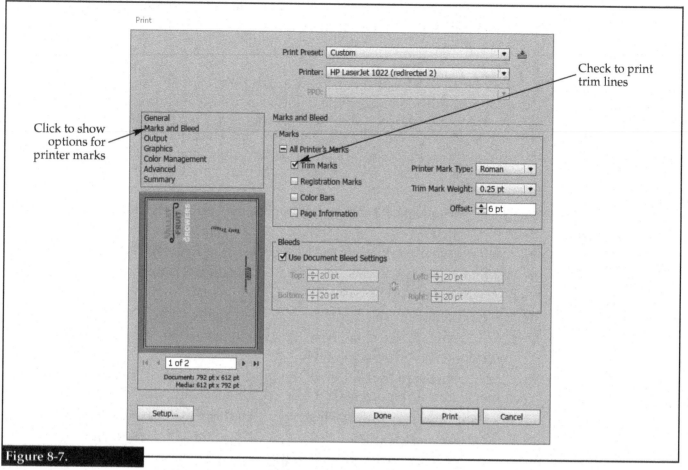

Figure 8-7.

Setting printing options for printer marks.

83. Click the **Brush Libraries Menu** drop-down arrow in the panel, and click **Artistic>Artistic_Calligraphic** in the drop-down menu. The **Artistic_Calligraphic** panel is displayed. Calligraphic brushes simulate the nib (tip) of a calligraphy pen. The brush is usually oval and produces thick and thin portions of a line depending on the orientation of the brush tip. The brush stroke is drawn in the correct orientation along the center of the path.

84. Click the **5 pt. Oval** brush in the **Artistic_Calligraphic** panel.

85. Set the stroke color to black.

86. Zoom in on the title on the front cover panel on the Brochure Outside artboard.

87. Click to the left or right of the space between line one and line two, draw a curlicue shape, draw a line between the text, and draw an opposite curlicue on the other side to create a flourish, as shown in **Figure 8-8.** Notice how the flourish has a varying width based on how the brush was moved.

88. Click the **Selection Tool** button in the **Tools** panel, and select the flourish. The path around which the stroke is applied can be seen. Notice the path is always centered in the stroke no matter what the width is.

89. Applying what you have learned, draw another flourish on the front cover panel. Draw it diagonally from the lower left to the upper right of the open space below the title.

For individual use only—reproduction or duplication of this copyrighted material is prohibited.

Figure 8-8.

Creating a flourish with a calligraphy brush.

Calligraphic brush used to create a flourish

Type on a Path

Type on a Path Tool

Type Tool

A common technique in illustration is to have text follow the contours of a curved line. This effect is easy to create in Illustrator using the type on a path tool.

90. Click the **Type on a Path Tool** button in the **Tools** panel.

91. Click near the beginning of the flourish you drew below the title on the front cover panel. The cursor is placed on the path at the point you clicked.

92. Add the text Tasty Treats!, as shown in **Figure 8-9.** Notice that the stroke color has changed to None and the flourish itself is no longer visible.

93. Click the **Type Tool** button in the **Tools** panel, select the text on the path, and format it as Times New Roman or other serif typeface, bold, and 28 points.

94. Use the **Align Left**, **Align Center**, and **Align Right** buttons to the right of the **Paragraph** link on the **Control** panel to see how the alignment changes the position of the text on the path.

95. Save your work.

Copyright Goodheart-Willcox Co., Inc.   For individual use only—reproduction or duplication of this copyrighted material is prohibited.

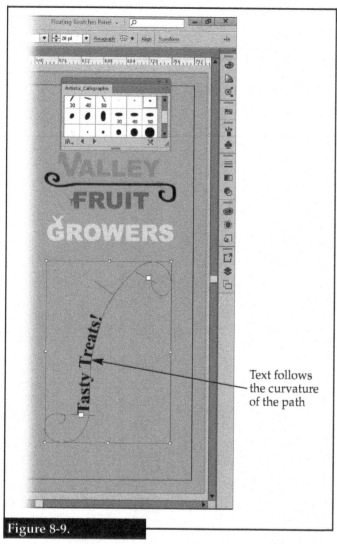

Text follows the curvature of the path

Figure 8-9.

Text can be fitted to a curved path. Afterward, the path is no longer visible except when the text is selected.

TIP
The New Document Profile folder may be located within a path that is hidden by default. You may need to turn on the display of system files and folders in order to see the folder.

Save a Template

The basic brochure template for the Valley Fruit Growers company is complete. However, to this point, you have been working in an Illustrator document file. Now it is time to create a template file.

96. Click **File>Save as Template...** on the **Application** bar. A standard save-type dialog box is displayed, however the default folder is automatically the Templates folder and the default file type is Illustrator Template (*.ait).

97. Name the template file *LastName_*FruitBrochure, and click the **Save** button.

98. Close the file, but leave Illustrator open.

99. Applying what you have learned, start a new Illustrator document based on the *LastName_*FruitBrochure template. Notice how all elements you added to the template are available in the new document, but the template file itself is not opened. Any Illustrator document started based on this template will contain these same elements.

100. Close the new document without saving it.

101. With the *LastName_*Brochure document open, click **File>Save As...** in the **Application** bar.

102. Navigate to the New Document Profile folder for Illustrator. The location of this folder will be different depending on your computer, its operating system, and where Illustrator is installed. The default location in Windows 10 is c:\Users*username*\AppData\Roaming\Adobe\Adobe Illustrator 20 Settings\en_US\x64\New Document Profile.

103. Save the file as Brochure_Profile.ai in the New Document Profile folder. Accept the default settings in the **Illustrator Options** dialog box.

104. Close the Brochure_Profile document.

105. Begin a new document. In the **New Document** dialog box, click the **Profile:** drop-down arrow. Notice Brochure_Profile is available as a profile. Any Illustrator file saved in the New Document Profile folder will be available in this list and can be used to populate the settings in the **New Document** dialog box.

106. Click the **Cancel** button to abort creating a new document.

For individual use only—reproduction or duplication of this copyrighted material is prohibited.

Copyright Goodheart-Willcox Co., Inc.

Package a File

When sending a file to the printing company, it is best to package the file so it includes all of the fonts and assets used to create the document. Packaging a file allows another user to get an exact copy of your work even if he or she does not have the fonts you used.

107. Open the *LastName_*Brochure file in your working folder.

108. Click **File>Package...** on the **Application** bar. The **Package** dialog box is displayed, as shown in **Figure 8-10**.

109. Click the **Choose Package Folder Location** button (folder icon), and browse to your working folder.

110. Click in the **Folder name:** text box, and enter Brochure_Folder (this may be the default entry). A subfolder with this name will be created in the folder specified in the **Location:** text box.

111. In the **Options** area, check which features to include. For this example, check all of the check boxes.

112. Click the **Package** button to create the package. If a warning appears describing appropriate usage of fonts (typefaces) under copyright law, read the message, click the **OK** button.

113. When the package has been created, a message appears indicating this. Click the **Show Package** button in the message to view the contents of the Brochure_ Folder folder in the default system file explorer.

114. Close the system file explorer, and close Illustrator.

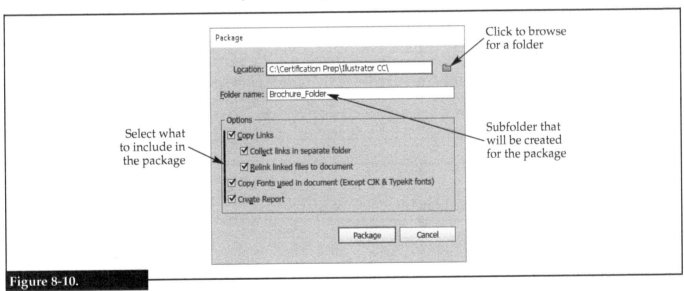

Figure 8-10.

A file can be packaged to ensure all typefaces and assets used in the document are available to another user.

Copyright Goodheart-Willcox Co., Inc.   For individual use only—reproduction or duplication of this copyrighted material is prohibited.

Lesson 8 Review

Vocabulary

In a word processing document or on a sheet of paper, list all of the *key terms* in this lesson. Place each term on a separate line. Then, write a definition for each term using your own words. You will continue to build this terminology dictionary throughout this certification guide.

Review Questions

Answer the following questions. These questions are aligned to questions in the certification exam. Answering these questions will help prepare you to take the exam.

1. Discuss the use of Greeked text.

_____

_____

_____

_____

2. What is boilerplate copy?

_____

_____

_____

_____

3. Explain the difference between tracking and kerning.

_____

_____

_____

_____

4. How is text converted to a vector image?

_____

_____

_____

_____

5. List the steps needed to make text wrap around a graphic.

_____

_____

_____

_____

For individual use only—reproduction or duplication of this copyrighted material is prohibited.   Copyright Goodheart-Willcox Co., Inc.

6. What is the function of trim lines and fold lines?

_____

_____

_____

_____

7. Describe how to open a brush library.

_____

_____

_____

_____

8. What happens to a path when text is fitted to it?

_____

_____

_____

_____

9. What type of file is saved from Illustrator with the .ait file extension?

_____

10. Describe how to start a new document based on an Illustrator template.

_____

_____

_____

_____

11. How can a designer make sure the printing company uses the correct typeface for an Illustrator document even if its computer does not have that typeface currently installed?

_____

_____

_____

_____

12. Briefly describe how an opacity mask is created using an oval shape and a portrait photograph so the interior of the oval shows the photograph.

_____

_____

_____

_____

Copyright Goodheart-Willcox Co., Inc.   For individual use only—reproduction or duplication of this copyrighted material is prohibited.

13. Which color in an opacity mask will fully hide and which color will fully reveal?

_____

_____

_____

_____

14. What does selecting a color setting (**Edit>Color Settings...**) do?

_____

_____

_____

_____

15. Which function or command is used to create a new document profile?

_____

_____

_____

_____

For individual use only—reproduction or duplication of this copyrighted material is prohibited.

Copyright Goodheart-Willcox Co., Inc.

Answers

Lesson 1

1. Shape, form, line, color, value, space, and texture.
2. Regular shapes and objects that are used to assemble more complex shapes or objects.
3. The primary colors of red, blue, and yellow.
4. A complementary color is located opposite of the selected color on the color wheel, while an analogous color is located next to the selected color.
5. Positive space is the area or volume occupied by the primary objects, while negative space is the area or volume around or between the primary objects.
6. The point or points in a perspective drawing where receding parallel lines appear to meet.
7. Movement, emphasis, harmony, variety, balance, contrast, proportion, pattern, and unity.
8. Movement.
9. Emphasis.
10. Balance.
11. An image is divided into three sections horizontally and three sections vertically to create nine areas, and where the lines cross are the focal points for a scene.
12. Contrast.
13. Unity.
14. To achieve site-wide consistency.
15. Shorter development time, easier maintenance, and improved usability.

Lesson 2

1. PNG-24
2. GIF, PNG-8, PNG-24, JPEG, BMP, and RAW or CIFF. (There are other file types.)
3. CGM, AI, and EPS. (There are other file types.)
4. RGB color model at a resolution of 72 or 96 dpi.
5. The alpha channel allows for a masking color, which is a single shade of a color that determines areas of transparency in the image.
6. Vector.
7. The process of converting a vector image into a raster image.
8. Raster images are composed of colored dots at specified locations, while vector images are composed of elements recorded by their mathematical definitions.
9. Applying the most appropriate resolution and file compression, which is a process known as optimizing.
10. Download it from a digital camera.
11. The image is dithered, and the software creates a color through interpolation.
12. 576

For individual use only—reproduction or duplication of this copyrighted material is prohibited.

13. Bicubic for enlargement.

14. A serif font has decorations called serifs at the ends of letters, while a sans serif font lacks these decorations.

15. Sans serif.

Lesson 3

1. Preproduction, production, testing, and publication.

2. Selecting the best team members for the job, identifying the tasks, and determining deadlines for that project.

3. Client goals and target market.

4. Using little or no text, including fantasy characters, and applying bright colors.

5. Demographics help segment the population into smaller groups that have similarities, which allows the designer to create items to appeal to the target market.

6. A drive-through restaurant will likely have a medium to low formality; examples will vary.

7. Raster images, because each point of color is recorded.

8. Working CMYK

9. Adobe Creative Cloud, CS Review, and Adobe Bridge.

10. A linked image maintains a connection to the original image file, whereas an embedded image is a copy of the image with no link to the original file.

Lesson 4

Figure 4-7

1. **Selection Tool**
2. **Direct Selection Tool**
3. **Group Selection Tool**
4. **Magic Wand Tool**
5. **Lasso Tool**
6. **Pen Tool**
7. **Add Anchor Point Tool**
8. **Curvature Tool**
9. **Type Tool**
10. **Type on a Path Tool**
11. **Line Segment Tool**
12. **Spiral Tool**
13. **Rectangle Tool**
14. **Polygon Tool**
15. **Flare Tool**
16. **Paintbrush Tool**
17. **Blob Brush Tool**
18. **Shaper Tool**
19. **Join Tool**
20. **Eraser Tool**
21. **Rotate Tool**
22. **Scale Tool**
23. **Width Tool**
24. **Crystallize Tool**
25. **Free Transform Tool**
26. **Shape Builder Tool**
27. **Perspective Grid Tool**
28. **Mesh Tool**
29. **Gradient Tool**
30. **Eyedropper Tool**
31. **Measure Tool**
32. **Blend Tool**
33. **Symbol Sprayer Tool**
34. **Line Graph Tool**
35. **Artboard Tool**
36. **Slice Tool**
37. **Print Tiling Tool**
38. **Zoom Tool**

Figure 4-8

1. **Color**
2. **Color Guide**
3. **Color Themes**
4. **Swatches**
5. **Brushes**
6. **Symbols**
7. **Stroke**
8. **Gradient**
9. **Transparency**
10. **Libraries**
11. **Appearance**
12. **Graphic Styles**
13. **Asset Export**
14. **Layers**
15. **Artboards**

For individual use only—reproduction or duplication of this copyrighted material is prohibited.

68. 288 points wide, 216 points high

107. 576 points high, 288 points wide

136. 72 points high, 216 points wide

145. 252 points

152. 36 points wide, 36 points high

154. 108 points in both **H:** and **W:** text boxes

167. 108 points

Review Questions

1. An artboard is where the images you create will be placed. All of the artboards in a document are placed on the canvas. You can also draw on the canvas, but only the content of an artboard can be saved as an image or printed.

2. A workspace is the layout of the toolbars, panels, and document on the screen.

3. The weight, or width, of the stroke is increased from 1 point to 9 points.

4. Click in the **Stroke Weight:** text box on the **Control** panel, and enter 6 pt.

5. The list in the **Layers** panel represents the stack of layers. The layers at the top of the list appear above the layers at the bottom of the list.

6. Click the **Toggle Visibility** button (eye) to the left of the layer name in the **Layers** panel.

7. Click the None swatch located in the upper-left corner of the panel.

8. Calligraphic, scatter, art, bristle, and pattern.

9. **View>Smart Guides**

10. Harmony rules are defined in the software to determine which will provide the best complement to a selected color. The harmony rules are used in the **Color Guide** panel.

11. Shades are darker than the active color, while tints are lighter.

12. Double-click the pattern swatch in the **Swatches** panel, and then use the tools available in the **Pattern Options** panel in pattern-editing mode to alter the pattern.

13. Click the **Artboard Tool** button to enable editing of the artboards, and then drag the artboards around the canvas as needed.

14. The new artboard will be the same size as the artboard that was selected in the panel.

15. The upper-left corner of the active artboard.

16. It is used to join multiple shapes into a single shape with only the outline of the new shape retained.

17. The number of shapes created between the selected objects to create the blend.

18. By double-clicking the button for the tool in the **Tools** panel.

19. By clicking the workspace switcher on the **Application** bar, clicking **New Workspace...** in the drop-down menu, and entering a name in the **New Workspace** dialog box.

20. In the **Preferences** dialog box accessed by clicking **Edit>Preferences** and then a submenu option in the **Application** bar.

Copyright Goodheart-Willcox Co., Inc.　　　　For individual use only—reproduction or duplication of this copyrighted material is prohibited.

Lesson 5

20. 1 inch wide by 1-2/3 inches high

Review Questions

1. Primitives are basic shapes, while a composite shape is a shape composed of multiple primitives that are arranged and stacked to form a complex shape.

2. (answers will vary) The viewer will combine the shape of the mouth with other visual cues, such as the positions of the eyelids, to determine the overall expression of the character; thus the whole face is greater than the sum of its parts.

3. Create a symbol from the group.

4. Select the symbol, and click the **Edit Symbol** button on the **Control** panel. Then modify the symbol as needed. Finally, click the **Exit Symbol Editing Mode** button to save the changes.

5. By clicking the **Break Link** button on the **Control** panel when the symbol is selected.

6. Adobe Flash

7. A dialog box is displayed in which the parameters of the shape can be set. When the dialog box is closed, the shape is automatically drawn based on the parameters.

8. By anchor points or nodes and control points. The location of these points and the distance control points are from the curve determine the shape of the curve.

9. The Bézier curve will have fewer anchor points and the shape will have smooth curves, whereas the line segment tool can only approximate a smooth curve with straight line segments.

10. In Illustrator, an ellipse is a type of Bézier curve. Its shape can be modified by using the **Direct Selection Tool** button and changing the positions of its anchor point and control points.

11. They show where the printed page should be trimmed (cut).

12. It creates a filled-in shape where the designer moves the cursor and then adds a stroke around the fill.

13. By using the stroke drop-down arrow on the **Control** panel when the compound path is selected.

14. Select all shapes to be mirrored, and then click **Object>Transform>Reflect...** on the **Application** bar. In the **Reflect** dialog box, select the axis about which to mirror the shapes.

15. Display the panel menu in the **Swatches** panel, and click **Select All Unused** in the menu. Then, click the **Delete Swatch** button at the bottom of the panel.

Lesson 6

81. Two inches (144 points ÷ 72 points per inch = 2 inches)

Review Questions

1. Click any color swatch in the RGB color group in the **Swatches** panel, and then click the **New Swatch** button to display the **New Swatch** dialog box. Define the new color in the dialog box.

2. Each gradient stop defines a color in the gradient. The position of each stop controls the transition from one color to another.

3. An artistic technique in which the value of shadow and light are changed without regard for color along a shape to create the illusion of three dimensions.

4. To provide separation between the background and the object.

5. It provides a visual cue of where an object is in relation to a surface.

6. A linear gradient has the color transition in a straight line, while in a radial gradient the transition is in a circular pattern similar to the ripples created by dropping a pebble into a pond.

For individual use only—reproduction or duplication of this copyrighted material is prohibited.

7. In the **Gradient** panel, click the **Type:** drop-down arrow, and click **Radial** in the drop-down list.

8. Apply an extrude effect to the circle, change the **Position:** setting, and enter 4 inches (or the equivalent in the current units of measure) for the **Extrude Depth:** setting.

9. X, Y, and Z

10. Z

11. In the **Appearance** panel, click the **Toggle Visibility** icon next to the name of the effect.

12. The effect must be accessed using the **Appearance** panel.

13. It simulates a realistic view by representing receding lines converging at a vanishing point or points.

14. Click the **Perspective Grid Tool** button in the **Tools** panel.

15. Click **View>Proof Setup>Working CMYK** on the **Application** bar.

16. A proof for printing must represent the four process colors of cyan, magenta, yellow, and black, while a proof for screen display must represent the colors used by monitors, which are red, green, and blue.

17. In the dialog box displayed for setting JPEG options, click the **Color Model:** drop-down arrow, and click **CMYK** in the drop-down list.

18. Click **File>Export>Export As...** on the **Application** bar, and set the **Save as type:** to **BMP**. In the dialog box that is displayed for setting BMP options, click the **Color Model:** drop-down arrow, and click **Grayscale** in the drop-down list. Also, click the **Resolution:** drop-down arrow, and click **Screen (72 ppi)** in the drop-down list.

19. Click **File>Export>Export for Screens...** on the **Application** bar, and make the appropriate settings in the **Export for Screens** dialog box.

20. It is in JPEG image format at the highest quality setting. The JPEG image format is a compressed file type that is suitable for use on websites.

Lesson 7

Review Questions

1. Placing

2. The pen tool because it allows both freehand curves and straight lines to be drawn in a single session of the tool.

3. Use the direct selection tool to select the anchor point, and then click the **Convert anchor points to corner** button on the **Control** panel.

4. Click the drop-down arrow to the right of the **Image Trace** button on the **Image Tracing** panel on the **Control** panel, and select the number of colors to use for the tracing in the drop-down list.

5. Place the photograph, draw the star shape over the image using black fill and no stroke, select the image and the shape, and click **Object>Clipping Mask>Make** on the **Application** bar.

6. A gradient mesh is like a net placed over the shape, and color transitions from each mesh point to its neighboring mesh points, whereas a standard gradient is applied in one direction only.

7. Use the direct selection tool to select and drag the mesh point.

8. To create smaller files that will load faster on a website.

9. As soon as the work is in tangible form.

10. The file can be freely used without asking permission from the owner; the copyright has been removed or has expired.

Copyright Goodheart-Willcox Co., Inc. For individual use only—reproduction or duplication of this copyrighted material is prohibited.

Lesson 8

Review Questions

1. Greeked text, or *Lorem Ipsum*, is dummy text not composed of real English words. It is used so attention is focused on reviewing the design instead of reading the words on the page.

2. Placeholder text that is intended to be used as is without alteration.

3. Kerning is the spacing between pairs of letters, such as A and V, while tracking is the spacing between all characters.

4. Select the text, and click **Type>Outlines** on the **Application** bar.

5. Select the graphic, and click **Object>Text Wrap>Make** on the **Application** bar.

6. These are printer marks that show the printer where to fold and trim the printed sheet.

7. Display the **Brushes** panel, click the **Brush Libraries Menu** drop-down arrow in the panel, and click the brush library to open in the drop-down menu.

8. The stroke color is changed to None and the path is no longer visible.

9. An Illustrator template file.

10. Click **File>New from Template...** on the **Application** bar, and then browse to and select the template file.

11. Save the Illustrator document as a package, including the typeface.

12. Place the image, draw the oval over the top of it filled with white, select the image and the shape, and click the **Make Mask** button in the **Transparency** panel.

13. White fully reveals and black fully hides.

14. It enables a particular color model to ensure the Illustrator document matches it.

15. The **Save As** function or command, and save the file in the New Document Profile folder.

For individual use only—reproduction or duplication of this copyrighted material is prohibited.